THE
SKY
AND
THE
PATIO

THE SKY AND THE PATIO

AN ECOLOGY OF HOME

Don Gayton

NEW STAR BOOKS
VANCOUVER
2022

NEW STAR BOOKS LTD
No. 107–3477 Commercial St., Vancouver, BC V5N 4E8 CANADA
1574 Gulf Road, No. 1517 Point Roberts, WA 98281 USA
newstarbooks.com · info@newstarbooks.com

Copyright Don Gayton 2022. All rights reserved. No part of this work may be reproduced, stored in a retrieval system or transmitted, in any form or by any means, without the prior written consent of the publisher or a licence from Access Copyright.

The publisher acknowledges the financial support of the Canada Council for the Arts, the British Columbia Arts Council, and the Government of Canada.

Cataloguing information for this book is available from Library and Archives Canada, www.collectionscanada.gc.ca.

Cover design and typesetting by Oliver McPartlin
Printed and bound in Canada by Imprimerie Gauvin, Gatineau, QC

First printing October 2022

Don Gayton

Contents

The Sky and the Patio 9
The Army of Five Hundred 19
The Beauty of Forced Reassembly 29
Andrew Douglass and Dendropyrochronology 35
Eocene Walk 47
Sagebrush, Science and Shifting Mosaics 53
Compost Fetishism and the Dirty Dozen 63
Cowboy Dreams 73
A Paean to the Sockeye 81
Giving Nature a Voice 93
Shambala, Feminization and Great Green Furballs 107
Places of Attachment 113
Chinook Wawa 123
Johann Wolfgang von Goethe and the Bee Balm 127
The Singularity of Frivolous Purpose 131
The Enduring Pleasures of the Woodstove 145
Turtle Naivete 153
The Natural History of the Bookshelf 161
The Pantheon of Dusty Heroes 169
Climate Change 173
Aliens, Golf and the Trout Creek Ecological Reserve 181
A Nagging Wish for the Divine 191
Mythmaking on the Similkameen 197
Chopaka Kilpoola Kobau 203
Patio Adieu 211

Suggested Reading 215
Acknowledgements 21

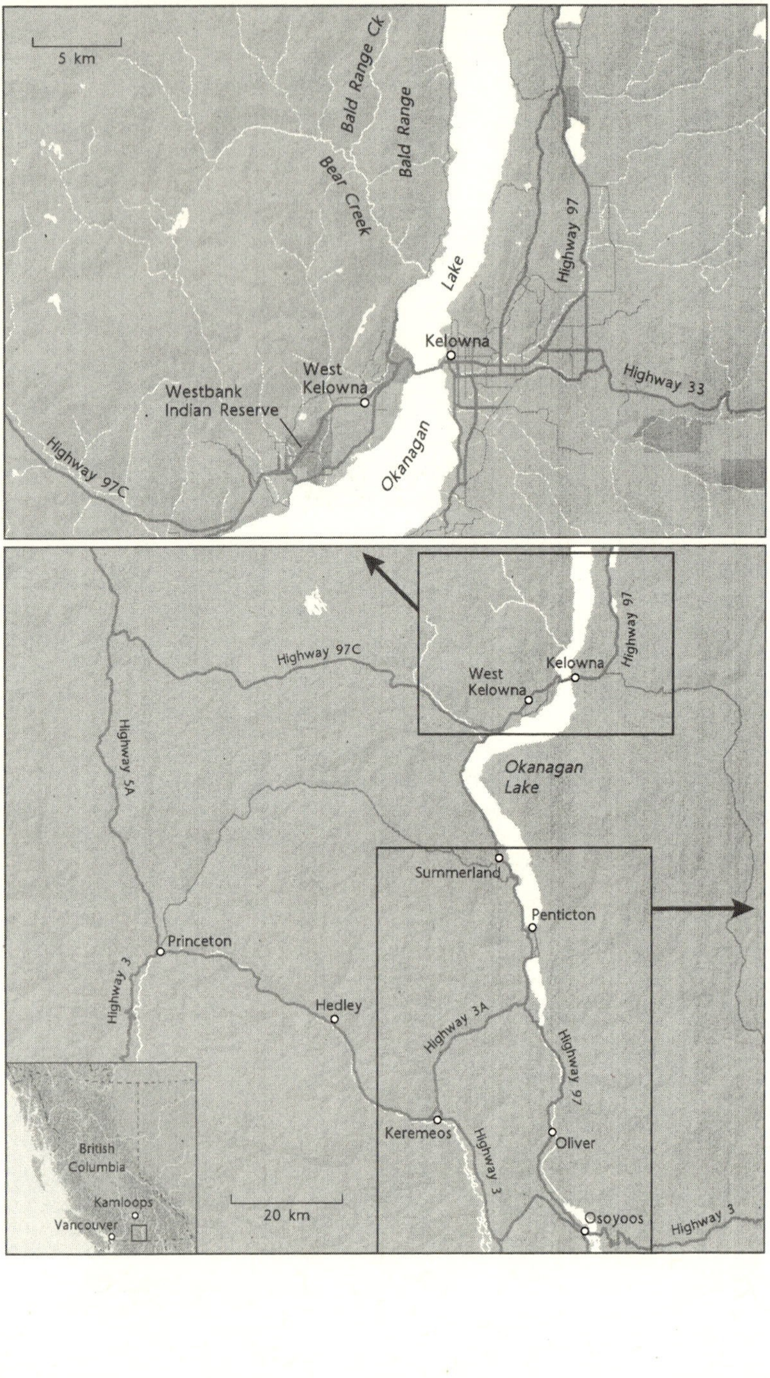
5 km
Bald Range Ck
Bald Range
Bear Creek
Lake
Highway 97
Kelowna
West Kelowna
Westbank Indian Reserve
Highway 33
Highway 97C
Okanagan
Highway 97C
Kelowna
Highway 97
West Kelowna
Okanagan Lake
Highway 5A
Summerland
Penticton
Princeton
Highway 3
Hedley
Highway 3A
Highway 97
Keremeos
Highway 3
Oliver
Osoyoos
Highway 3
20 km
British Columbia
Kamloops
Vancouver

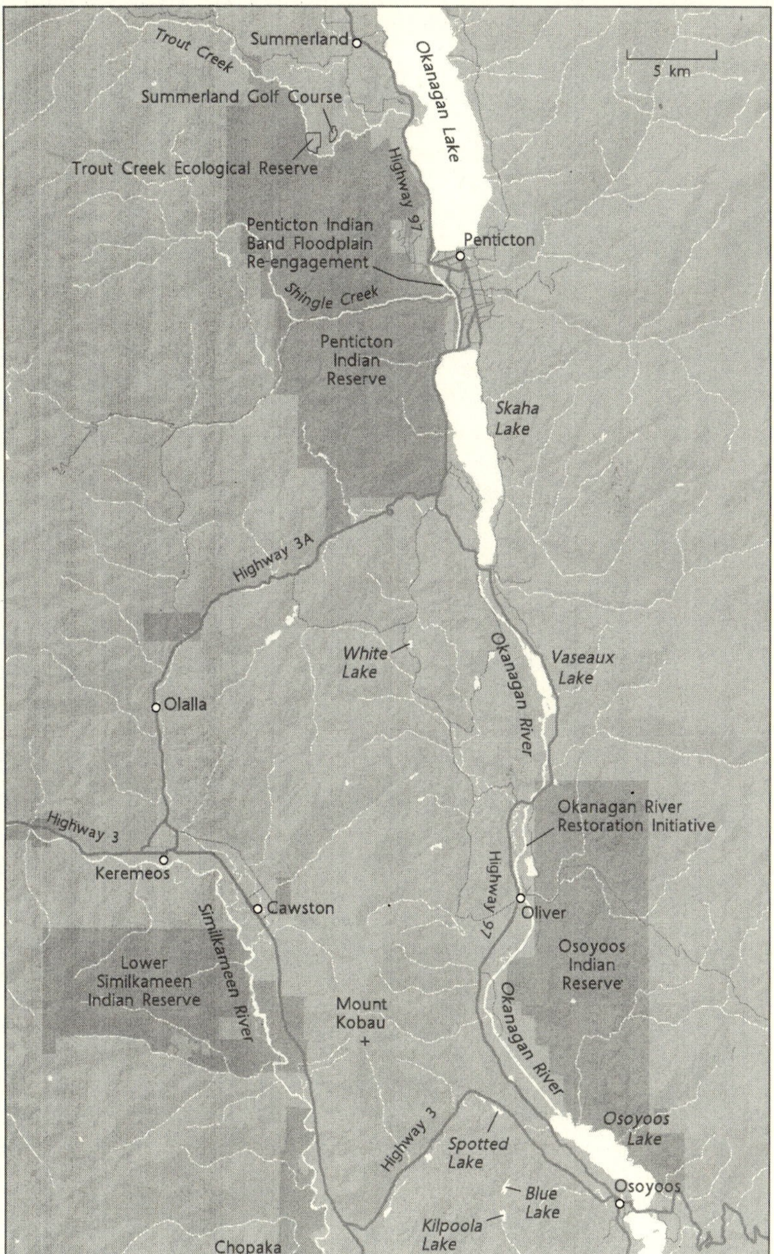

Summerland
Trout Creek
Okanagan Lake
5 km
Summerland Golf Course
Trout Creek Ecological Reserve
Highway 97
Penticton Indian
Band Floodplain
Re-engagement
Penticton
Shingle Creek
Penticton
Indian
Reserve
Skaha
Lake
Highway 3A
White
Lake
Okanagan River
Vaseaux
Lake
Olalla
Okanagan River
Restoration Initiative
Highway 3
Keremeos
Highway 97
Cawston
Oliver
Similkameen River
Lower
Similkameen
Indian Reserve
Osoyoos
Indian
Reserve
Mount
Kobau
Okanagan River
Osoyoos
Lake
Highway 3
Spotted
Lake
Osoyoos
Blue
Lake
Kilpoola
Lake
Chopaka

1
THE SKY AND THE PATIO

EVENING CLOUDS MOVE like an immense, quiet army, all dressed in purple and gold. They march steadily northward over the top of nearby Conkle Mountain. It is April, and I am consummating my first outdoor patio supper of the year, under this referential sky. It is a full auditory evening: hungry coyote pups yip from somewhere on Conkle, as they anxiously await mother's return from her hunt. Neighbourhood dogs respond in kind. Then cheers go up for a home run at our small town's softball field. Pacific tree frogs in a slough nearby add their separate chorus. Earlier in the day I heard the season's first sandhill cranes: harbingers of oncoming spring. These great birds are heard long before they are seen, on their migratory journey from Texas to Alaska. Yard work comes to a halt while you (literally) crane your neck to look for them. Sandhills are always far higher in the sky than first assumed. Sometimes you don't see them at all because they are flying *above* the clouds. But they do return, every April, and I am humbled by that.

I am confident the natural forces that govern the lives of sandhill cranes, coyotes and tree frogs also compelled me onto our patio this first spring night.

To name this space a *patio* seems a bit out of place. The word has Mediterranean or at least Californian overtones, and here I am in British Columbia's Okanagan Valley, eighty kilometres north of the forty-ninth parallel. But a patio, in fact, is what this is: a safe, enclosed outdoor space adjacent to a house, specifically designed for leisure. An inner court open to the milder elements, and to ideas. An outdoor room, if you will. A half-hidden garden. Right

The Sky and the Patio

now I might be sitting here wearing a down parka and mukluks, but it's still a patio.

Our own humble patio specimen has a high wooden fence on the street side, a cedar hedge on the neighbour's side, a grape arbor on the backyard side, and a door into the kitchen on the house side. Roofing materials consist of sky and clouds. The ground surface is paving stones on one half, and dandelion-infested grass for dogs and grandkids on the other. The grape arbor is a single massive vine of Coronation, a table grape variety developed right here at the Summerland Agricultural Research Station. I have trained the vine into two double cordons, one above the other. The dark, twisted trunk, together with the outstretched and bare cordon arms, somehow reminds me of those rakishly thin Giacometti statues. Additional haphazard patio landscaping includes an ironwood tree, a clematis and some volunteer daffodils. And in summer my wife, Judy, festoons the place with hanging baskets of grocery store ornamentals. Furniture consists of a sturdy aluminum table and mismatched lawn chairs. Other items are some incandescent string lights overhead, a bit of statuary, a propane barbecue and a little wall fountain with an electric pump. Food and books are often brought from the house to the aluminum table. Everything is low-budget, but at the same time, priceless.

The word *patio* is nominally from the Spanish language, but the word's linguistic roots go far back into Old Provençal and Latin, signifying variously "a communal pasture," "a covenant," or "to lie open." The Arabic equivalent is the enclosed courtyard or *fana'*, and the patio concept appears in many other building styles and cultures. Our patio functions as a human communal pasture when we gather there with friends to enjoy food, wine and conversation. The long Covid shutdown reminded us just how life-sustaining that companionship is.

A patio is a refuge, but one that is exposed and slightly daring. Perhaps it is a tacit acknowledgment that we humans have spent more evolutionary time outside than inside. To my mind, the

The Sky and the Patio

Argentine poet Jorge Luis Borges (1899–1986) captured the patio's fundamental essence when he wrote:

*El patio es el declive
por el cual se derrama el cielo en la casa*

The patio is the channel
down which the sky flows into the house

I do like this Latin connection, particularly when I am enjoying an Argentine Malbec or an Italian Sangiovese. But right now, after a winter of reds, I am acknowledging spring with a fruity Okanagan Chardonnay. Wine certainly does lend itself to multiculturalism.

Over the winter I experiment with various inexpensive red wines, including my own, eventually settling on two or three favourites. Then, come spring, I start the same process with whites. The beauty of this two-phase system is that the vagaries of memory and retail availability mean we experiment afresh every fall and spring.

This inaugural spring evening reminds me that the patio is my symbol and launching pad for a personal connection to nature. That connection is not a duality; it is, in fact, a reciprocation. Really a triumvirate, or a tripling. In between the distinct entities of humans and nature lie such enterprises as forestry, agriculture, fisheries, landscaping, gardening, eating and drinking, all of which attempt some collaboration with the natural world. A patio is a welcome refuge, but also a point of real and virtual departure to natural places both local and distant, followed by welcome return. Human history figures in as well. The patio is the sum total of what we make of place — of our home place, together with our home bioregion. To be on the patio is to lie open.

This home valley hosts the Okanagan River, one of eight major tributaries of the sprawling Columbia River system. The upper two-thirds of the Okanagan's length are in British Columbia, the lower third lies in eastern Washington State. The Canadian portion of the Okanagan's valley is narrow and deep, but there is minimal elevation loss as the waters flow southward, so "river"

The Sky and the Patio

here consists of six large lakes with short riverine connections in between. Okanagan towns and cities occupy the lowlands between those lakes, and the openings to side valleys. Just to the west of us lies a sister river, the Similkameen, which joins the Okanagan just south of the US border.

These two valleys, on both sides of the border, are the current and ancestral home of the Syilx (Okanagan) people. Many of our place names, including Kelowna, Penticton, Keremeos, Osoyoos and Okanagan, are anglicizations of the original nsyilxcən words. The seven bands of the Okanagan Nation Alliance play a major role in managing these two valleys' wild parts.

The forty-ninth parallel, from Hope to the Alberta border, is a revealing thousand-kilometre cross-section of southern British Columbia. Aside from the seven major valleys — the Fraser, the Similkameen, the Okanagan, the Kettle, the Columbia, the West Kootenay and the East Kootenay — the rest is all mountain. Even from within these valleys, mountains loom closely on either side.

The landforms I look at every day are products of ancient volcanism and plate tectonics, further sculpted by Ice Age glaciers and meltwater, then overlain by dryland trees and grass, and finally colonized by upscale suburbs. Over the top of the patio fence to the southeast I can see the peak of *kɨtpus* or Giant's Head, a dormant volcano which at some point in geological time was casually tossed on its side. The imposing rawness of its cliffs and rockfaces is sullied by the designer homes on its flanks. To the southwest is Conkle, falsely pretentious since it is really not high enough to be called a legitimate mountain. Then to the west of us is a long, low ridge, another minor product of this region's tortured geological history. The ridge is dry and grassy, with scattered pines here and there. Fortunately, it is too steep to build houses on — yet. From the perspective of leisurely patio evenings, I scan this ridge, speculating on the fundamental duality of Okanagan ecology: trees and grass. Forest and grassland. The tree that grows here is the hardy ponderosa pine, which reaches farther out into dry grasslands than any other species. The dominant native bunchgrass that grows here is the stately bluebunch wheatgrass. Ponderosa and bluebunch are locked into a complex and seesaw relationship that spans ten thousand years, in rough numbers.

On the ridge's lower slope I can see the three-dimensional bulk of each tree as well as the evening shadows they cast on the grass below them. But the trees that line the ridge itself are two-dimensional, seen only in profile. With late-day light behind them, they have the look of black-and-white illustrations in old forestry textbooks. Very few have the classic Christmas tree shape; most are funky and asymmetrical. Life as a tree in this dry, windy habitat does not make you pretty. So this ridge hosts a rogue's gallery, a police lineup, of deviant pines. Some look like they have stood since the glaciers; others appear new, temporary or even rudely invasive. When evenings are longer and supper is done, it is fun to pour more wine and begin assigning names to various trees on the ridgeline. There is the Beanpole, the Bonsai, and the Lightbulb. Dead Top, Leaning Left, Charlie Brown, Windswept. Witch's Broom, Schoolmarm Crotch. Then there is Filigree, and Basho Inspiration. Crooked Way to Heaven. Overbloated. Aspirational. Calligraphic. And so on. You get the drift. The portion of the ridgeline that I can see hosts several dozen of these trees, so none of my names are permanent, and they shift over time and drink. The two exceptions are an ancient, nearly branchless snag standing next to a healthy and perfectly symmetrical individual. Those two are permanently named Moses and the Teenager.

The ponderosa pine's role in our Okanagan ecosystem does not end when it dies. Standing dead snags carry life onward as habitat for cavity-nesting birds, raptors and bats.

Ponderosa is not my first iconic tree. As a kid living in Southern California, I befriended a large old pepper tree, which became a personal refuge and gymnasium. Its sturdy trunk and spreading main branches were perfect for climbing. The weeping terminal branches hung vertically around the tree's outer perimeter, creating a large, shaded canopy. It was a quiet, pepper-scented room, with a plush carpet of duff below and pure adventure above. On one of

The Sky and the Patio

my more daring climbs I lost my grip and fell, landing flat on my back in the duff. Unconscious for a few seconds, I opened my eyes to the sunlit and radiant tree canopy. I was mildly interested in what had just happened, but totally overwhelmed by the beauty of the infinitely complex mosaic above me: a mass of delicate pinnate leaves shot through with light. That may have been a transformative moment.

Trees not only evoke memories, they contain them. The nearby White Lake Formation bears fossil remnants of the metasequoia, iconic tree of the Eocene age, when our climate was lush and subtropical. The ponderosa itself remembers fire, carefully encoding it in scars and tantalizing us with the possibility of revealing the conditions and drivers of past eras.

The long needles of the ponderosa are coated with a very thin layer of transparent wax. The wax helps prevent water loss, but it also reflects sunlight. Sit down under a mature ponderosa on a midsummer afternoon when there is a breeze blowing, and look upward through the foliage. You will see thousands of tiny points of moving light. Naturalist John Muir did this a century and a half ago, as he gazed up at the enormous ponderosas of California's Sierra mountains.

A sudden flight of unknown songbirds passes through the patio and is gone again, in less than a heartbeat. Another group — English sparrows is my uneducated guess — arrives to stay in the yard momentarily, each selecting a different perch. Then, of course, there are the small flocks of California quail that forage through the neighbourhood. They are simultaneously the silliest and most endearing of Summerland's wild creatures. Very ground-based birds, these quail overcome heavy domestic-cat predation by raising two or even three large broods every summer. Quail do love their dust baths: any areas of dry, bare ground in the yard will always have rounded depressions where these birds have indulged their habit. Quail craters, I call them.

Tonight's patio meal is sockeye salmon fillets, pan-seared. I am an indifferent cook, but I have devised a marination in a mixture

The Sky and the Patio

of Quebec maple syrup, soy sauce and lemon juice, followed by a pan fry that is hot, fast and messy. The challenge is to blacken the salmon skin without welding it to the bottom of the pan. At the appropriate moment, one surgically inserts the spatula between the skin and the flesh, separating the fillet but leaving the skin stuck to the pan. Then lift the fillet, reverse it and lay it back down precisely on its skin, to fry the second side. It is custom work. The blackened skin seems like a pleasant way of participating in the carbon economy. Once the fillet is nearly ready, I pour in the surplus marinade and reduce it down to a thick sauce to pour over rice or sop up with bread.

After finishing a glorious patio meal, I often speculate about living solely on salmon, perhaps combining it with other regional foodstuffs like saskatoon berries (*siya*) and bitterroot (*spitlum*). But that musing is quickly put aside: the lovely pink flesh I just consumed belongs to a species facing extinction, at our own hands.

My wife's job has her out of town during the week, so when I eat alone on the patio, I like to read as well. This activity takes some thought and preparation. One of my supper reading accessories is a pair of what I call book blocks, one to support the upper edge of the book for a better reading angle, and another to lay across the top of the pages being read, to hold them in place. This latter block is particularly important as we tend to get evening katabatic winds, as cool air coming off the western mountains slops down to our warm valley bottom. You do have to give credit to the verboleptic meteorologists who coin such delightfully obscure words like *katabatic* and *noctilucent*.

I made my first book blocks out of some lovely maple I had in my shop. Thinking they should be elegant as well as practical, I sanded them with increasingly fine grit and then applied a nice finish of Swedish oil. Mistake. They were far too slippery. I would be just nicely settled into my reading when the top block would slide down the page and land on my blackened salmon. So I abandoned the elegant maple blocks and substituted a couple of badly weathered pieces of SPF two-by-four (*SPF* is industry code for "spruce, pine or fir"). The other essential patio supper reading accessory is a tea towel thrown over your shoulder, so you can wipe residual grease and fish skin off your fingers before you turn pages.

Selecting the appropriate book also requires some forethought, since there are many options. Continue with the novel you are currently engrossed in. Choose something at random from your bookshelf. Try a book you have been avoiding, knowing your commitment to it only has to last as long as the evening meal. Bring a backup selection, in case the first one doesn't strike your literary fancy.

Food and wine pairing is a well established but rather highbrow tradition. Can the evening's book choice also pair appropriately with the food and wine — a tripling, so to speak? I experimented with that notion for a while, but gave it up as too exacting. Now I am content with simply good food, a decent wine and an interesting read. None of these are particularly hard to find, and it is remarkable how often they synergize.

Tonight's book selection was a toss-up between William Jordan's *The Sunflower Forest* and Paul St. Pierre's *Smith and Other Events: Tales of the Chilcotin*. I chose the Jordan book, a fundamental statement of the philosophy behind ecological restoration.

Jordan reasons that we humans need to feel humble in the face of a higher power, we need to feel shame, we need to give, and we need rituals. These elements have traditionally been met by organized religion, but the role of the church in contemporary society has diminished substantially, leaving those needs largely unmet. What better substitute, Jordan argues, than ecological restoration (ER)? Doing this work, we can feel humble in the face of the infinite complexity and beauty that is nature, we can acknowledge the damage we have done to it, and we can do the restoration work with no expectation of monetary return. As for ritual, ER projects replicate the time-honoured activities of research, planning, preparing, planting, tending and monitoring. Interesting, but I think ER cries out for more than that — it needs rituals of performance: music, dance, theatre, spoken word.

The Sky and the Patio

Jordan goes on to say that our North American approach to nature is personal, citing Henry David Thoreau and John Muir as classic examples of the individual bonding with nature. While not rejecting this approach, Jordan argues for creating communal bonds with nature as well, and offers the group activity of ecological restoration as an ideal venue for this.

I look back on some of my own ER experiences, and they don't quite match up with Jordan's compelling vision. Many were kind of Arbor Day exercises, where we would spend a few hours planting potted native trees or shrubs, feel good about ourselves, and leave our plantings to their own devices. Most would then die from either lack of water, deer browsing or smothering by weeds. One other ER attempt I was involved in, a more ambitious project on an abused piece of federal land, was smothered by government bureaucracy.

It is late now on the patio, fully dark except for my reading lantern. The great horned owl makes his presence known. He occupies an enormous Douglas-fir at the end of our block. His late evening recitations are hauntingly melancholy, so different from those of daytime songbirds. I listen for a while and then go back to the Jordan book. Turning the page, I discover a delicate pencil tick mark next to a passage that moved me during a previous reading. I am, of course, deeply offended when other people treat books this way — a used bookstore find ruined by orange magic marker underlining — but the tiny pencil mark is my best compromise between respect for books and losing track of memorable passages. This Jordan tick mark was about his concern for "the depth and extent of the human regard for the natural landscape."

I raise my greasy glass to that.

2
THE ARMY OF FIVE HUNDRED

KILLING WEEDS IS a fundamental human activity, along with procreation and violence. I reflect on our many herbicidal strategies as I dig dandelions in the scruffy kids-and-dogs yard next to the patio. The digging is a pleasant springtime activity, creating the illusion of real progress, at least until the next morning. But as spring advances, I grow weary of this Sisyphean exercise. The dandelion, *Taraxacum officinale,* has so many ways to beat you. Some strains flower early, others late. Some produce flowers as tiny seedlings, others postpone flowering until middle age. All of this genetic diversity can be found within a single backyard. Once a dandelion's taproot is firmly anchored, it actually contracts, pulling the plant's crown downward into the soil, out of harm's way. And, of course, each puffball releases half a gazillion seeds, each equipped with its own parachute.

Some people go after dandelions on hands and knees, but I use a single-bladed stand-up digging fork. I keep the V-shaped blade of the fork very sharp, and revel in the sound of fleshy taproots being sliced clean through. Manufacturers of household implements casually ignore the needs of left-handers and tall people, so I make adjustments. My digging fork has been fitted with an extra-long handle, thus reducing lower back stress and providing a better posture for thinking about the disturbing, fascinating world of alien invasive plants, while killing them one by one. This little patch of suburban grass has its share of weeds: dandelions, round-leaved mallow, morning glory, storksbill, creeping bellflower, quackgrass — all the usual suspects. Weeds favour edges to establish and grow in, so the smaller the planted space, like this one, the greater the edge influence becomes. Even though philosophical reflection is my normal bent, it is hard to stay on the metaphysical plane while being confronted with the latest bozo eruption of some new weed in our yard, or in our valley. Where exactly was that one, solitary, individual pioneer species that I missed identifying and killing last year, which somehow produced enough seed to carpet the entire yard with its progeny this year? There is some historical evidence to suggest that weeds took down the entire Aztec civilization, by decimating their corn crops. I can relate.

For us ecologists, invasives are like the reciprocal of species at risk. The adaptive traits that weeds possess are mostly not shared by rare species, and vice versa. Plant responses to soil disturbance and to soil nitrogen are two such traits. Invasives establish rapidly on disturbed ground, and they are typically gluttons for nitrogen. Natives, and particularly the rare natives, generally have slow reproductive and establishment rates, and can do quite well in nitrogen-poor soils. Soil disturbance is a double delight for invasives, since it opens up new niches at the same time as it exposes roots and dead plant material to soil microbes, who busily break them down, producing lots of available nitrogen in the process.

Plants become weeds when they travel. The arrival date and rate of spread of new invasives is another topic to ponder. Dandelion didn't come from its native Europe to North America on the *Mayflower*, but almost. Early settlers brought it with them for medicinal and food purposes, and by the mid-1600s it was well established in eastern North America. Then the durable little monster accompanied settlers as they moved west. Dandelion found very congenial niches in pastures and farm fields, suburban yards, gardens, parks, ball fields and roadsides, and never looked back. Plant distribution maps typically show green polygons where a plant is found, and white where it is not. With the exception of a few desert, alpine and boreal areas, the dandelion map for North America is totally green.

Bulbous bluegrass, another European species, has a different immigrant story. It was a government introduction, as a potential turfgrass, in 1907. The earliest Okanagan record for this species is from 1974, and then a few more isolated occurrences in the 1980s. Beginning in 2016, a local population explosion occurred, and within three years it became the dominant roadside grass in this valley, even crowding out another highly successful invasive, cheatgrass. Nobody knows why. Bulbous bluegrass is unique in that it produces bulbs rather than seeds. I was stunned by this hostile takeover, but I won't miss picking the nasty, pointy seeds of cheatgrass out of my socks. However, I am sure the next nasty invasive is somewhere in the queue, ready to outperform bulbous bluegrass.

The means by which the seeds of plant invasives have arrived — and continue to arrive — on this continent are legion. Contaminants in hay, grain or other crop seeds. Manure of animals transported internationally. Packing materials. Conscious introductions by well-meaning horticulturists, or immigrants bringing a nostalgic bit of the old country in their suitcases. Herbalism has been a huge source of invasives; before modern pharmaceuticals, every ailment had a corresponding plant remedy. My own European ancestors put great store in these various herbs, and when they immigrated, they brought seeds of their favourites with them.

I wonder about the fate of some of our iconic Okanagan ecosystems. Do we, for example, acknowledge that our storied native grasslands are now "heritage ecosystems" since nearly all of them now contain non-native cheatgrass, knapweed and toadflax? The same with our wetland and streamside native, reed canarygrass, now largely replaced by the much more aggressive European strain? One of the great ironies of invasives is this: the poorer the soil and growing conditions, the fewer the invasives. On my walks through the grasslands, I frequently come upon "balds" — areas with a thin layer of dry soil over bedrock. These are small universes of mosses and lichens, with a scattering of tough and resilient native broadleaves, and few, if any, invasives.

Invasive weeds spawned the chemical herbicide industry, which has grown to the point that it is now central to industrial agriculture. The case can be made that certain herbicides are necessary for farming, but they are certainly far less essential for our lawns. Yet every hardware store, feed store and big-box store carries an impressive selection of weed killers, ammunition for our all-out lawn war on dandelions. As I walk by those malodorous store aisles, I like to paraphrase the immortal words of Robert Duvall in *Apocalypse Now*: "I love the smell of 2,4-D in the morning."

The Monsanto corporation went to the trouble of gifting us with a proprietary, genetically modified strain of canola, which was immune to the effects of Roundup, Monsanto's chemical herbicide. Some may remember the epic legal battle between Monsanto and Percy Schmeiser, a Saskatchewan farmer. The mega-corporation accused Schmeiser of growing their GMO canola without permission, even though he never seeded it. Monsanto's lawyers cleverly ignored the fact that canola is a wind-pollinated crop, and GMO pollen from an adjacent field had crossed with Schmeiser's non-GMO canola, seed from which he used to grow a subsequent crop. It is testimony to the power of multinational chemical corporations that Monsanto actually won their case in court.

Mechanical control of weeds is Sisyphean and chemical control is soul-destroying. But there is a third option. Biological control, commonly known as biocontrol, is a new entrant in the endless X Games of weed suppression. Biocontrol is also all about travel. Take some ordinary plant native to a place like Europe, Kazakhstan or Japan, and imagine it as the harassed single parent of a large and quarrelsome family. Suddenly, it is swept away on a permanent overseas vacation, leaving all the meddlesome in-laws, difficult children, unwelcome guests and toxic neighbours behind. This is a key reason plants become weeds: they arrive in the new country without any of the beetles, moths, leafcutters, root borers, sapsuckers and seed eaters that, back in the old country, keep them in check. The essence of biocontrol is to go back to that home country, search out the pests of that plant, and bring them over to spoil the vacation. Biocontrol is a kind of e-harmony for bugs.

I worked on the margins of biocontrol for several years, including sharing a small office in Nelson, BC, with one of the discipline's early pioneers, Val Miller. Often, I would arrive at work in the morning only to find all available space, including my desk, cluttered with containers full of the latest creepy-crawly.

My first actual hands-on biocontrol experience happened on the Bald Range, an open, grassy mountainside tucked in among the ponderosa pine forests west of Kelowna. Elegant bunchgrasses and hardy balsamroots abound there. Native bees and other insects attend to the flowers while, overhead, solitary raptors work the thermals. The Bald Range is a landscape well suited to epiphany, but its humble beauty has been defaced. Historical overgrazing, fire suppression and all-terrain vehicles have each left their legacy of damage, and they have synergized with each other to produce an even more destructive whole. Part of the Bald Range's legacy of damage is a truly spectacular infestation of a noxious alien weed known as Saint John's wort, known in the US as Klamath weed (*Hypericum perforatum*).

This European weed, brought here originally as an herbal medicine, is common in many parts of BC and the western US. Populations of this plant are typically small and scattered, due to a highly successful biological control insect known as Chrysolina. The poster child of weed biocontrol, this insect was the first to be purposefully released in North America, in 1944. Chrysolina is a lumbering, iridescent, Volkswagen-shaped beetle that looks like it just crawled off the pages of a children's book about bugs. It was brought to BC in the early 1950s and it became a very successful immigrant, spreading its progeny throughout the southern half of the province. The beauty of Chrysolina is its voracious appetite for Saint John's wort and its total disdain for any other plant. Such a one-on-one relationship is not unique in nature. The classic of this genre is soapweed yucca, found in southern Saskatchewan, and its pollinating partner, the yucca moth. Neither can reproduce without the other.

The theory of biocontrol is elegant and simple, but its execution is complex, time-consuming and expensive. Once an identified candidate insect is collected from its native habitat, a batch is sent for a lengthy stay in Switzerland, the home of an international biocontrol consortium. There, the insects are placed in a sealed greenhouse with dozens of plant species, from azaleas to zucchinis, but no host plant. Then the critters are closely watched for several years. If they so much as nibble on a non-host plant, they are immediately drummed out of the program and sent back to Kazakhstan, and another candidate insect is brought in. Once the Swiss scientists can finally verify that a particular insect actually starves and dies without its host plant, they move on to the next phase, where techniques of mass rearing are developed. Then comes the final phase: precious containers of the new candidate insect are sent to various locations in British Columbia, where the host invasive plant is plentiful. These releases are then watched closely for some years, to determine success or failure. The entire process typically takes two or three decades; most introductions end in failure, but the Chrysolina beetle is a wonderful exception.

As a habitual visitor to the Bear Creek Bald Range (one must be specific — BC has several Bald Ranges), I was acutely conscious of its Saint John's wort infestation, which in places made up ninety percent of the vegetation, displacing bunchgrass, balsamroot, and pretty much everything else. But oddly, there were no Chrysolina attackers. This particular beetle is easy to spot, due to its big, iridescent black body, but several close inspections of the Bald Range during peak season revealed not a single insect. This was strange, since the beetle is considered well established by provincial authorities and can be found everywhere its host plant is found.

So I added this observation to my list of Bald Range questions and curiosities, and carried on. But as the years passed, it became obvious that the Saint John's wort infestation was spreading, and spreading rapidly. Saint John's wort is a well-known herbal remedy for mental depression, and I figured we now had enough Bald Range biomass to cheer up several provinces and territories.

I put a call in to an old colleague, Catherine MacRae, an invasive plant specialist with the Ministry of Forests in Nelson, BC, to see if there was a chance of getting a few beetles. She told me the Chrysolina was experiencing one of its periodic down cycles, and few were available for capture and re-release. But she promised to keep my request in mind. A few weeks later, Catherine's technicians found a burgeoning bug population near Nelson, and I got an urgent notice that five hundred beetles were coming via the overnight express bus to my hometown of Summerland.

Early the next morning, I met the bus as it pulled in to the station and — no bugs. Frantic and knowing the beetles can experience high mortality from even short shipping delays, I called Catherine. She gave me the tracking number and I contacted every depot on the bus route between Nelson and Summerland. No luck. "In transit" was the standard unhelpful answer. The Bald Range's chances for a Chrysolina rescue were fading fast. I waited two anxious hours, made the round of phone calls again, and finally discovered that the bug shipment had been mistakenly delivered to the Kelowna bus station. That station's freight clerk reminded me that it was Saturday morning, that they were closing in about forty-five minutes and wouldn't reopen until Monday. I made an instant calculation: it was an hour's drive from my house to the Kelowna bus station, and every bug would be dead by Monday.

Pedal to the metal on Highway 97, my ancient Ford Explorer smoking from overexertion, I had visions of my beetles dying slow, excruciating deaths in the Kelowna bus depot warehouse. But somehow the gods of Kelowna's out-of-phase traffic lights smiled on me, and I sailed right through to the north-end bus station, where the package awaited. The warehouse person was not pleased to hear that the box was full of insects, and he very reluctantly loaned me his razor knife to open it. Inside, carefully packed in vented plastic containers, nestled in Styrofoam noodles and sharing a cold pack, were five hundred live, active insects. I thanked the apprehensive warehouse man profusely, and made a beeline, or rather a beetleline, for the Bald Range.

To get to the Bald Range, you drive twelve kilometres up the dusty washboard of Bear Creek Road, then a kilometre up a narrow spur road, followed by a steep ten-minute hike to get onto the Bald Range itself. I did that in record time. As I left my car, I transferred the bug containers from the box into my backpack. Heading up the hillside, I began to worry that my black backpack was acting as an unintentional solar oven, and the bugs would overheat and die on the very last leg of their epic journey. So I did a forced-march hike in record time. Arriving at the middle of the Saint John's wort infestation, I was relieved to see the bugs were still active in their containers. Now I faced a dilemma that I hadn't thought of before. Where was the best place to put the bugs? In a dry spot, a wet spot, a spot with young plants, or an area with mature plants? In the end I decided on five separate locations, each slightly different, and marked them with my trusty GPS for future reference.

My Chrysolina release was one of the handful of acts of random ecological beauty one gets to be a part of in a lifetime. This delivered beetle population may, in their insect wisdom, take to the Bald Range, or they may reject it and die off. After all, they were many kilometres, generations and ecosystems removed from their home country of England. One very plausible outcome of my release: the beetles will be successful, but the niche that Saint John's wort formerly occupied will get filled by another alien species, from our foul and burgeoning cornucopia of new invasive weeds. But we must take satisfaction in small victories, as we keep fighting the larger war.

Gently emptying these bugs from their containers was the culmination of a very long ecological and personal loop. Now I was embracing the full irony of biocontrol — introducing a new alien species to control an existing alien species. Exactly the kind of delicious dilemma that keeps me immersed in the discipline of ecology.

Most of my tiny, iridescent army of five hundred came out of their containers easily, but there were a last few I had to coax onto my finger and then place onto carefully chosen Saint John's wort leaves, one beetle per plant. Those last few holdouts seemed genuinely grateful, and so was I.

3
THE BEAUTY OF FORCED REASSEMBLY

DOMESTIC LANDSCAPING SELF-REGULATES. Drive down any residential street and you see the rules, all firmly self-enforced. Lawns, hedges and flower beds all laid out in proper order. Everything rectilinear, with the occasional perfect oval. Breaking rules is a personal habit of mine, but the notion of landscape dissent never occurred to me, until I was forced into it. This is how it happened.

Half of our Okanagan backyard was once occupied by a neatly organized vest-pocket vineyard. I developed it under the tutelage of my friend George, an accomplished viticulturist and viniculturist. Drawing on his Latvian heritage, he had learned every chapter in the great book of wine, and he took me under his wing. He provided me with cuttings of Zweigeltrebe, a robust Austrian red wine grape. George felt this variety (usually abbreviated to *Zweigelt*) was a good one for me to start with. Making halting steps over the first few years, I realized the problems of my sixty-vine vineyard, discounting economics and scale, were not that different from a ten-thousand-vine enterprise. Getting to know other home grape growers and winemakers in our small town, I found a common thread of humility. These folks have to learn a wide range of cultural practices, grape varietal characteristics, watering schedules and vinting techniques. They must also be able to convert every new problem into a fascinating learning experience. Otherwise, it is far easier to just go to the local liquor store.

Over the years, I faced various vineyard problems, including a nasty powdery-mildew attack and a voracious gang of starlings.

The Sky and the Patio

But my little cottage industry carried on, yielding a few cases of drinkable Zweigelt every year. Growing grapes and making wine is the ultimate geezer enterprise, since there is always some little thing that needs to be done, like tying up a rogue cane that has broken free from its trellis, thinning excess grape clusters, fixing an irrigation leak, or racking last year's vintage.

This viticultural trivia was replaced by major gravitas when we decided to build a carriage house on our suburban lot, to accommodate boomerang children. This meant moving more than half of the vineyard. Fortunately, it was late winter when the house decision was made, giving me time to fret, research and plan before I had to face the challenge. Serious questions loomed: would my vines survive transplanting? What would the root system of ten-year old grapevines look like? How deep, how wide would the roots extend? How much root mass must I capture for the vines to survive? Digging into the literature — my instinctive response to most situations — I found the work of Cato the Elder. Besides being a conservative Roman senator, historian and obsessive moralizer ("patience is a virtue"), he was also a farmer. His very specific instructions in *De Agricultura* for transplanting wine grapes were as follows:

> Dig them up carefully, roots and all, with as much of their own soil as possible, and tie them up so that you can transport them. Have them carried in a box or basket. Be careful not to dig them up or transport them when the wind is blowing or when it is raining, for this is especially to be avoided. When you place them in the trench, bed them in top soil, spread dirt over them to the ends of the roots, trample it thoroughly, and pack with rammers and bars as firmly as possible; this is the most important thing.

Pretty sound advice, considering it was written 2,300 years ago. They say that wheat was the first agricultural crop. I'll bet wine grapes were not far behind.

Looking into somewhat more contemporary research literature on grapevine rooting patterns, I discovered that $Y = (1 - d)$. Interesting theoretical approach, but not very helpful. Further reading uncovered a "profile wall" study, where the scientists (read: underpaid grad students) dug a trench adjacent to an established vine and then recorded the location of every single exposed root, most of which were found radiating outward and downward at between 10 and 150 centimetres below the soil surface. Typically, there were a few strong laterals interspersed among a vast array of tiny feeder roots. In the stony, unforgiving soil of my yard, I knew I would be lucky to get a root ball that was even fifty centimetres deep, but my vineyard mentor George reminded me that in spite of all the highbrow esoterica we ascribe to wine, grapevines themselves are tough, almost weedy plants.

Trellising is another wonderfully complex aspect of viticulture, and was also part of my transplant worry. Of the dozen or so different trellising systems, George recommended the double-cordon arrangement. With this system, each vine has a vertical trunk and two permanent horizontal cordons, forming a T shape. Each cordon, about a metre long, produces four or five annual fruit-bearing "canes," which grow up vertically from buds on the cordons. The canes then get pruned off after fall harvest, and a new set of canes emerges from the cordon buds the next spring.

Transplanting entire vines with their cordons intact seemed too much to ask of these traumatized, root-poor transplants, which would have to supply water and nutrients to eight or ten buds. Hedging my bets, I cut the cordons off each side of the trunk, just beyond the first buds. If everything worked out, I would gently train the expanding buds to become the new replacement cordons. And then the next year I would be back to my original double-cordon/upright-cane system.

I was now ready to transplant, emotionally and scientifically. And it was time to face an issue I had been avoiding: where to put the forty vines that had to be moved. Our large house lot had given me the immense privilege of dividing it up into four separate spaces.

One was a backyard which suffers from Lumpy Lawn Syndrome, where we would play sports like off-road bocce and free-range badminton. The second was an area of random shrubs and small trees. The third was a garden plot with tomatoes and cannabis. The fourth was a native plant garden. Emotionally attached to all these spaces, I was not prepared to sacrifice any of them, so there was no alternative but to integrate the new vineyard right into their midst. So I laid out the new vine rows, snaking them in between established ginkgos, flowering almonds, saskatoons, peaches, antelopebrush, Kentucky bluegrass and Maui Wowie. Unprecedented arrangements previously unknown to either landscaping or viticulture. Plant pairings I would never have conceived of, until I was forced to.

Scientific and emotional preparations complete, armed with a sharp, curved shovel called a "drain snake," I started my first early spring vine extractions. As I plunged the shovel downward, I could hear it slice through the thumb-thick laterals, a truly cringe-worthy sound. This must be how the surgeon feels while cutting through flesh: wincing, but knowing it is in the best interest of the patient. But perhaps I was anthropomorphizing too much.

Vine rows are typically spaced about two metres apart — the optimum trade-off between sun penetration and yield per hectare. As I transplanted, I stuck fairly close to this measure, but left one very wide row to preserve the full length of our bocce court. As I started to dig holes for the transplants, it occurred to me that I was not the first to integrate grapevines with domestic landscaping: Italians and Greeks have been doing it for centuries, adding architecture into the mix as well. Those folks were not forced to do so as I was; they did it willingly, and with elegance. So I took heart.

Garden, both noun and verb, is a delightfully ambiguous term, and it stands at the very centre of my domestic reassembly. Historically, the garden has aristocratic overtones. Picture men in wigs and ladies in formal dresses passing idle afternoons among the manicured shrubbery, sipping from Delft teacups, and lamenting the difficulty of finding good servants. At the other extreme are the community gardens of today, where contemporary landless urban peasants are able to get their hands dirty and produce a few vegetables. Such a garden thrives on Vancouver's East Hastings Street, probably the most troubled neighbourhood in the entire country.

The lawn has a similar dichotomy. Historically, it represented privilege, a public statement that I, owner of said lawn, am so affluent I can put this productive land to purely ornamental use, rather than growing cows or cabbages upon it. On the other hand, the modern lawn represents a democratic departure from the walled estate, which was hidden from public view. Open to the street, the lawn invites casual encounter and neighbourliness. We water and weed our front lawns partly from necessity, and partly from the desire for human contact.

How does one separate the term *gardening* from the term *landscaping*? Answer: one doesn't.

My grape transplants survived, likely due to cool and forgiving spring weather, rather than my extensive research and performance anxiety. Our previously compartmentalized yard is history: now I contend with overlapping conceptual ambiguities of landscaping, ornamental gardening, food gardening, native plant culture, turfgrass management, cannabis production and viticulture. The vine rows, those normally bland and boring strips of grass between the rows, now have an eclectic mix of yarrow, squash and creeping buffalograss, a curious native from Saskatchewan.

Terroir is a wonderfully fuzzy wine term, a combination of soil science, climate, tradition and sheer creativity. It connects wine to place. My own backyard terroir has been a mix of suburbia, aspirational inexperience and riverstone. I shouldn't discount the zucchini influence.

I do love reading the effusive language on wine labels, and aspire to be a wine label writer. Here are a few I have written, as a practice exercise:

> This cheeky Pinot Gris woos you with its in-your-face fruitiness and saucy finish. Perfect for an afternoon of extreme croquet.

The Sky and the Patio

A wine robust enough for two men to drink, after they have pissed into the radiator of an overheated 57 Chev flatbed, in the desert, under a full moon.

For those who admire unoaked Auxerrois, Ambling Armadillo 09 arrives at the absolutely apropos enological aperture.

A red blend with unexpected glissandos, yet dark with troubling undercurrents. A wine to turn Rodney Dangerfield into a philosopher, Albert Camus into a standup comic.

As I contemplate the results from our patio, I see positives from this forced reassembly. Now I am back in my happy place of dissent, thinking outside the rigid rule boxes of landscaping, grape growing and gardening. In the future, my wine may have grace notes of carrot and a bouquet of antelopebrush.

4
ANDREW DOUGLASS AND DENDROPYROCHRONOLOGY

PONDEROSAS DOT THE hillside beyond our patio, but this resonant pine has a role at the table as well. Cork hotpads are standard for dinner tables, but I have fashioned one from ponderosa pine. It is a cross-section that I cut from a mid-sized tree, about two inches thick. Like the book blocks, I have sanded it smooth and treated it with Swedish oil. This tree "cookie" is like an open book for those who wish to read it. Each tree growth ring chronicles a year in ecological time.

Tree rings link to astronomy, archaeology, and ultimately, to fire. This is how it happened.

In 1894, a young Harvard astronomer made the impetuous decision to move to Flagstaff, Arizona, to join wealthy astronomer Percival Lowell at his new observatory. Flagstaff was a cowboy town at the time, remote from Ivy League centres of celestial study. However, it was at high elevation and boasted incredibly clear nights, perfect for telescope work. This young Harvard man, Andrew Douglass, was attracted to sunspots. He theorized these periodic solar disturbances were connected to variations in the earth's climate, and he was looking for historical data to support his theory. The paltry few decades of available weather records were not enough for Douglass; he needed a long-term "weather surrogate" in order to test his theory. One day, as he rode a buckboard through the dry forests near Flagstaff, he found his surrogate. It was the cut stump of an old ponderosa pine.

The Sky and the Patio

We all remember from high-school biology that most tree species produce annual "growth rings" just under the bark. The inner boundary of each ring is made up of thin-walled, light-coloured cells that grow during the flush periods of spring and early summer, and the outer boundary is composed of thick-walled, dark cells produced in late summer and fall. The thickness of each annual growth band is a crude measure of that year's seasonal precipitation. Wet years produce wide rings, dry years narrow ones. This is particularly true for trees growing in dry climates, like that of northern Arizona.

As Douglass began to investigate tree rings, he built on knowledge that dates all the way back to (who else?) Leonardo da Vinci. The profoundly observant Leonardo was passing through the streets of Ravenna when he stopped to study the growth rings on a cut stump. Tree rings were noted again by the poet-botanist Carl Linnaeus in the mid-1700s, and a few decades later, dendrochronology (tree ring dating) became a fledgling science. As astronomer Douglass delved into dendro, he realized northern Arizona had not only clear nights, but also ancient, drought-stressed ponderosa pines exquisitely sensitive to local climate. His quest was over: the growth rings of these veteran trees were his long-term climate archive.

Elated, Douglass got to work building his theory that sunspots affect climate, as demonstrated by variations in tree growth rings. Along the way, he accomplished an astronomical first: photographing zodiacal light, that eerie "false dawn" caused by light reflecting off dust floating around the sun. He also quarrelled with his boss, Percival Lowell, who was convinced that Mars was inhabited by aliens.

In the midst of Douglass's lab work, he was interrupted by a local archaeologist, who wondered if tree rings in wooden beams from the ancient Indigenous Pueblo cliff dwellings could be used to date the time of their occupation. Douglass was both annoyed and intrigued. That rude interruption not only contributed to southwest archaeology, but it also forged the basis for documenting forest fire history and fire ecology.

Andrew Douglass and Dendropyrochronology

The basic mechanics of dendrochronology are deceptively simple: start with a freshly cut tree cookie, sand it down with increasingly fine grit until the surface is mirror smooth, and then study the rings. Count back from the bark to the centre ring, add ten years for the seedling stage, and you have the age of the tree. To correlate the rings to climate, you look for the very narrow rings produced by drought years, and wide ones by wet years. A ponderosa pine's rings offer up not only the tree's age, but also a rough summary of what each year's growth conditions were like.

Creation stories, even the prosaic ones, beg to be told. My first exposure to dendrochronology was in Cranbrook, a town in BC's Rocky Mountain Trench. The Trench is a hallowed, multi-generational battleground contested by ranchers and elk hunters, since both cows and elk graze the Crown grasslands and open forests of that spectacular mountain valley. As a newly fledged government range officer, fresh off the boat from Saskatchewan, I attended a contentious rancher-hunter meeting, intent on learning the particulars of this dispute. The accusations and counter-accusations were intense. Halfway through the meeting, a young man entered the room, pushing a handcart with an enormous tree slab on it. He waited patiently until the usual bombast settled down, and the chairman reluctantly gave him permission to speak. The young man pointed to one side of the tree slab, which had a large open "catface" where an initial fire had scorched through part of the bark but did not kill the tree. The next fire, and remarkably, every fire after that, had left its mark on the open catface. This tough old ponderosa pine had survived many fires, each one leaving a tiny scar in the growth ring corresponding to the year of the fire. The fellow explained that historically, the Trench had experienced frequent fire, which meant that trees were suppressed and there were lots of open grasslands, and plenty of forage for both cows and elk. "Why don't we join forces, get back to that historical fire frequency, and make more grass?" he suggested. "We can either keep on fighting each other for nothing, or work together and get paid for it."

The meeting went quiet for a minute while that eloquent piece of cowboy wisdom was digested. Some actual discussion ensued, but by then I wasn't paying attention. I was busy examining the tiny scars on the tree cookie, fascinated. Once a tree is scarred by a fire but not killed, subsequent fires will leave their mark on it. What a brilliant notion. A tree can be a record not only of climate, but of the historical incidence of fire as well. As I gently touched each scar, a new, fully-fledged obsession arose from my fingertips: dendropyrochronology, the cross-discipline of dendrochronology and forest fire science.

In a very small way, my revelation mirrored that of Andrew Douglass. A few months after the Cranbrook awakening, my wife Judy and I booked off to attend a week-long dendroecology workshop in Montana. This annual workshop, entitled the North American Dendroecoecological Field Week (NADEF), was a delightfully intensive mix of field work and microscope work. Our group, composed mostly of grad students, started off by hiking across a broad Montana mountainside, identifying fire-scarred trees and stumps. Then came chainsaw work, taking selected trees down and cutting cookies from them. Packing the cookies back to the lab, we then spent hours sanding, using progressively finer grits, until the surfaces were smooth as glass and the rings plainly visible. Then on to the final step, counting rings, measuring ring widths and identifying fire scars, using binocular microscopes. Non-scientist Judy enjoyed hanging out with the tree nerds and asking deceptively innocent questions like "Why are you doing that?" and "If you skip all the statistics, what does it really mean?"

A distinctly human foible is the ability to keep two highly compatible topics in separate parts of your brain, failing to connect them for months and sometimes years on end. Then some random short-circuit occurs, eliciting the response "Why didn't I think of that before?" Such a synapse occurred while I was hiking on one of my favourite local haunts, the Trout Creek Ecological Reserve (TCER), not far from our home. It is a lovely, dry, south-facing slope hosting a mix of ponderosa pine and native grassland. The synapse, likely prompted by sunshine and the faint but still pungent odour of pine resin, connected NADEF and TCER. Sure enough, in the space of one afternoon hike, I spotted several candidate trees and stumps bearing fire scars.

After securing permission from provincial authorities, I cut cookies from twenty-eight different trees and stumps on the ecological reserve. This was another free weight-loss clinic, scrambling up steep hillsides, chainsaw in hand, and then back down again with the cookies and the chainsaw in a backpack. After the requisite and uncounted hours of sanding and microscope work, I had a quite detailed history of fire on this small ecological reserve, dating back to the early 1700s. As I worked, I kept noticing a particularly well-preserved, elegantly fire-scarred cookie. When the project was finished, I stored the rest of the cookies in the shed and kept that one as a hotpad for our dinner table.

As I compared my Trout Creek results with other ponderosa fire history studies in the BC Interior and adjacent eastern Washington State, a remarkably consistent pattern emerged. Prior to European settlement, fires were quite frequent and generally small. The approximate scale of each fire can be determined by sampling several fire-scarred trees in a given area. If scars for a particular year only show up on a few trees, then we assume the fire was small; if a same-year scar appears on many widely dispersed trees, then the fire was likely a large (and hot) one. On a regional scale, seeing scars on many trees from the same year indicates a "fire year" when extreme summer weather conditions produced several large fires.

All the ponderosa pine zone studies I looked at identified a pre-settlement fire frequency (the "historical natural fire return interval," in nerdspeak) of five to thirty-five years. This means that on a given parcel of land, like the thousand-hectare hillside I can see from our patio, a fire would have occurred somewhere within that parcel every five to thirty-five years — most small, a few large.

Fire scientists have developed many ingenious monitoring methods, one of them being a means of remotely detecting lightning strikes, and then determining the percentage of those strikes that actually start fires. Applying the strikes-per-fire statistic to the pre-settlement era leaves a huge gap: there were not nearly enough lightning-caused fires to account for the typical five- to thirty-five-year fire frequency. Additional dendro work showed many of those pre-settlement fires occurring in early spring or very late fall, seasons when lightning is uncommon. The dendropyro data makes it abundantly clear that First Nations were actively using fire as a tool in pre-settlement times, a fact corroborated by oral tradition and by elders of many First Nation communities. It is logical to assume most of those shoulder-season fires were Indigenous cultural burns.

Our regional fire chronology tends to settle out into five distinct periods, with minor variations based on location.

One: the pre-European-settlement era, 1700–1880. During this time, First Nations used fire for enhancing forage for game and horses, for increasing food and medicinal plant growth, for improving defensive sightlines and for a host of other reasons. The practice is often referred to as Indigenous cultural burning. This period obviously extends several millennia before 1700, but our fire records do not: in this dry interior climate of cold winters and hot, dry summers, few trees live beyond 300 years.

Two: the colonial period, 1880–1920. First Nations were confined to reserves, their cultural burning practices were declared illegal, and the new influx of cattle reduced the amount of fine fuels available to carry fires, so fire incidence dropped dramatically.

Three: 1920–1940. This was a period of prolonged drought, which, combined with ignition sources from the new railway, mining and logging activities, produced some very large and destructive fires.

Four: the fire suppression era. Shortly after World War II, our ability to detect and suppress wildfires became highly effective. "Out by 10 o'clock" was the forest firefighter's mantra, and it resulted in several decades of comfortably minimal wildfire activity.

Meanwhile, our interior towns and suburbs expanded upward into forested hillsides.

Five: 2010 to the present. Heavy fuel loading resulting from decades of successful fire suppression combines with climate change to create a disturbing new era. There are a few halting attempts at reintroducing fire in the form of prescribed burns, but their scale is miniscule when compared with the size of the problem. The year this period started is open to some debate, but 2010 is a likely candidate. Collectively, we assume we are still in the fourth period, and these more frequent, more intense wildfires are a temporary aberration. That assumption is getting harder and harder to maintain.

Dating fires on a cookie cut from a live, fire-scarred tree is a laborious but relatively straightforward process of counting back from the current year ring, the one just underneath the bark. But there is another, tremendously valuable reservoir of historical fire data residing in fire-scarred snags and old stumps. The challenge with these is to determine when the tree died — was it ten, or seventeen, or maybe fifty-two years ago? There is no obvious way of telling. Here again, Andrew Douglass steps into the breach. He pioneered the concept of the "master chronology" for his archaeological work. The technique is now used in all aspects of dendrochronology, including dendropyrochronology.

Douglass's master-chronology method works like this. First, you map out the forest stand where you will be doing your fire history. Then you identify the dry ridges and knobs within that area that might host ancient, live trees. The trees you seek out are those that never experienced fire, and that never had any other source of moisture except precipitation, and are thus exquisitely sensitive to the local climate. Chainsaw in hand, you sacrifice one or two of these reference trees. Then you make several cookies from them in the lab and measure the individual ring widths. Next, you hand those cookies to an experienced colleague, who does the same procedure without reference to your own results. Then you jointly compare and correct. At the end of this process, you have a lengthy, fully dated master chronology for your study area. Now, since your undated mystery stump or snag is from that same area, you can assume it was subject to the same climate variations over time. Now you can compare the two chronologies, to look for a fit.

The standard method for doing the comparison is called skeleton plotting. Taking the master chronology, you generate a horizontal bar graph on a long strip of graph paper. Each vertical bar represents a year. The height of each individual bar is determined by ring width: narrow rings are given short bars, wide rings get tall bars, and the various gradations in between. You do the same thing for your undated mystery tree cookie, and then you place the two strips of graph paper — Master and Mystery — together on a table, with the long axes parallel to each other. On the Master graph, you choose a dramatic weather signature, say two wet years (tall bars) followed by three very dry years (short bars). Then you slide the Mystery graph back and forth until you find the equivalent weather signature. When the signatures click — and sometimes they never do, for a host of reasons — it is truly an epiphany. You and your fellow tree nerds dance in celebration in the lab, putting fragile binocular microscopes at risk.

Douglass continued his work on tree rings and sunspot cycles, but the unresolved question of the ancestral Puebloan cliff dwellings haunted him. From living pines in the area, he was able to develop a master chronology that extended back about 750 years. By collecting ancient roof beams, scrap wood and even bits of charcoal from the Pueblo cliff dwellings, he was able to create another chronology, but it was undated and floated mysteriously in time. He concluded that the mystery Puebloan chronology had to precede even the earliest beginnings of his dated chronology. Sunspots took a back seat as Douglass spent years looking for a wood sample that would establish a bridge between the two. Finally, he discovered a roofbeam at the Show Low ruins in east central Arizona that became his "Rosetta Stone." The beam's earliest tree rings fit his undated floating chronology, and its later rings fit the dated chronology. In a single stroke, that Show Low beam linked and extended Douglass's chronology by some 500 years, back to 1,250 years ago. As a result, he was able to fix the Show Low ruins as having been built in the late 1100s.

There is great value in misdirected obsessions; I know that not only from personal experience. There is also much to be gained from the profound mistakes of others. Astronomer Percival Lowell was sure he saw narrow canals on Mars, citing it as clear evidence of alien life on the Red Planet. It turned out the canals were ophthalmic: he was actually seeing blurry blood vessels in his own eyes. Yet in his canal quest, Lowell was responsible for significant advances in astronomy technique. Ecologist Frederic Clements was convinced that every ecosystem, given a long enough time, would evolve to a single "climax" suite of vegetation. He was proven wrong, but in the process he inadvertently spawned the discipline of ecological succession. Similarly, Andrew Douglass was never able to link climate variation to sunspot activity, but in the process he created breakthrough technology in the vastly separate discipline of dendrochronology. A contemporary scientist reviewing Douglass's work had this to say: "If we have no expectation of the [sunspot and tree ring] cycles observed, we are limited to confusion and chaos. Douglass had an expectation." His sunspot theory has faded into the background, but Douglass is now revered as a pioneer of modern dendrochronology.

Ecologists refer to repetitive natural events like floods, landslides and fires as "disturbances" that ecosystems have evolved not only to tolerate, but to actually depend upon. Ponderosa pine ecosystems are considered to be "fire-maintained," that is, they not only withstand fire, they derive certain benefits from it. Lodgepole pine ecosystems, which are common at higher elevations above the Okanagan Valley, are also connected to fire, but in an entirely different way. The short-lived lodgepole is known as "fire-dependent," since it relies on infrequent, large, hot fires to kill the existing stand and regenerate a new one.

When humans amplify, modify or eliminate a long-established natural disturbance, we call that action a "perturbation," something

The Sky and the Patio

ponderosa ecosystems have experienced now for several decades, as a result of fire suppression. Ecosystems typically do not respond well to perturbations. Ponderosa pine is pre-adapted to fire. It has thick, insulating bark, and the bark itself consists of loose plates that tend to fall off the tree as they burn. The tree self-prunes its lower branches over time, eliminating the "ladder fuels" that can propel a ground fire up into the tree canopy. A healthy ponderosa pine can withstand losing half or more of its needles to fire, and still survive. We assume all of these adaptations were in place long before humans entered the picture, but there is a strong overlap of ponderosa pine distribution with First Nations territories in the intermountain West. The ponderosa, plus the ecosystems that support it, adapted to Indigenous use of fire. This is where fire history intrudes into philosophy, making it all the more interesting. If an ecosystem experiences a human disturbance for long enough, does it evolve to depend on that disturbance? Such may be the case with Indigenous cultural burning in ponderosa pine ecosystems; over the millennia, that ecosystem type adjusted to their burning practices, so much so that our modern fire suppression now constitutes a perturbation. This throws a big monkey wrench into the standard view of nature as a whole and self-regulating system that has no need for humans, but which tolerates our impacts due to a superabundance of resources and built-in resilience.

British Columbia's Southern Interior has had its share of recent "fire years." Among them, 2003 and 2018 were notable, but 2021 dwarfed them both. My patio evenings that summer were dystopian: the setting sun was blood-red, bits of white ash drifted onto the table, and I could barely see the nearby ridgeline through the smoke. Twin-engine Convair airtankers flew low overhead, returning to the Penticton airport from retardant drops on multiple fires in the region. Then the single-engine Cessna skimmers arrived, seven flying in perfect unison, scooping water from Okanagan Lake and then circling to gain altitude before heading out of the valley. Helicopters slinging enormous water buckets took their turns. The summer's persistent heat dome was breathless. The lack of wind was a blessing for exhausted firefighters, but the heat and stillness always carried the portent of sudden, violent weather change.

My ponderosa pine hotpad, a feature of these evening patio meals, bears several fire scars, some dating as far back as the 1700s. Normally just an everyday household object, the hotpad took on symbolic significance during the 2021 fire year, reminding me of the paradox we residents and homeowners in dry forest ecosystems face: you can't live with fire, but you can't live without it.

We citizens of the Okanagan must find a way to embrace that paradox, and soon.

5
EOCENE WALK

A SHORT WALK through a tiny Kelowna neighbourhood has layers of meaning for me. This walk is routinely undertaken by our unspoken fellowship of cancer-centre patients who shun the expensive hospital parkade, and who don't mind the five-block walk to free neighbourhood parking. Another meaningful walk for me is in the White Lake Basin, about a hundred kilometres south. The two walks are separated by 50 million years, and joined by a tree.

During the Eocene epoch, the White Lake Basin and other parts of BC supported lush semi-tropical vegetation. The signature tree species of that epoch was metasequoia, also known as the dawn redwood. On my walks in this quiet, introspective basin, I have collected a few fossil samples of that tree's unique feather-shaped leaves. They are encased in light grey sandstone and perfectly preserved. The leaves themselves are jet-black, paper-thin precursors of coal.

I knew the fossil history of the tree but was totally ignorant of its contemporary role, until one of my cancer walks. Passing by an upscale home, I noticed an odd-looking tree in the front yard. The foliage, a kind of hybrid cross between needles and leaves, triggered a shock of recognition: was this actually a metasequoia? I was dumbfounded. In a brief trespass, I nipped off a single leaflet and carefully placed it in my pocket notebook. Returning home from the cancer centre, I went immediately to lay the fresh leaf alongside my fossil samples. Despite the intervening 50 million years, they were absolutely, and stunningly, identical.

After discovering that this ancient wonder *lived*, I delved into facts on the tree. Metasequoia was assumed by all to be long extinct until a Chinese botanist named Wang Zhan found a single grove of it in a remote corner of Sichuan Province in 1943. Samples were brought to North America, and subsequently the tree became a popular landscape specimen, particularly in the warmer parts of the US. Apparently, this was common knowledge to everyone but me.

There are a daunting number of subdivisions within Kingdom Plantae, but highlighting a few helps to illustrate metasequoia's unique position. It is defined as a conifer, or cone bearer. Conifers are all evergreen, with a few notable exceptions: larch, tamarack and metasequoia are deciduous, shedding their foliage every fall. Nearly all conifers have needle-like leaves except, not surprisingly, metasequoia.

The metasequoia has two coniferous evergreen cousins, the enormously tall coast redwood, found intermittently along the California and Oregon coasts, and the famous, long-lived giant sequoia of California's Sierra mountains. The scientific name of metasequoia is *Metasequoia glyptostroboides,* which of course is laden with meanings not accessible to us mortals. But the prefix *meta-* does speak to me. Its Latin definition is "beyond" or "transcendent."

The first person to describe metasequoia fossils in the BC Interior was George Mercer Dawson (1849–1901). Growing up in Central Canada, Dawson spent much of his short adult life exploring the Canadian West. An indefatigable traveller, geologist, anthropologist, writer and photographer, Dawson collected in the fossil-rich terrain around Princeton, BC, on the Similkameen River. He sent his fossil samples back to his father, Sir John William Dawson, professor of geology at McGill University in Montreal. Both father and son were eminent Canadian scientists, and their careers overlapped, in both time and interests.

This illustrious father, Sir John Dawson, was a bundle of contradictions. Broadly educated, progressive and an expert on fossil flora, he was also a devoted Presbyterian and staunch creationist, totally rejecting Charles Darwin's recent theories of the ascent of man from hominid ancestors. To the elder Dawson, a Darwinian human would be a repugnant, amoral beast, bent on destroying nature. In his increasingly desperate attempts to reconcile science and the Bible, he subscribed to "day-age creationism," which posited that each of the seven days of creation could have been thousands or even millions of years long.

Young George contracted tuberculosis of the spine as a child. The illness twisted his body and stopped its growth. As a result, he was probably not comfortable in society. Upon completing university, he spent most of the rest of his life in the Canadian wilderness. A prolific writer, he was also intensely private, and never once voiced an opinion on evolution. He did, however, reject formal religion. In one of his unpublished poems he mused:

> When alone I turn
> To where the lights of heaven burn
> My lips refuse to utter prayer

It is quite possible that profound ideological differences with his father motivated son George to spend most of his adult life roaming through Western Canada. By the time he was an adult, Darwin's theory was widely accepted, so it is counterintuitive to suppose the supremely rational George Mercer Dawson was a creationist. In one of his private notebooks, penned later in life, he wrote, "I live behind entrenchments and fortifications fancied by myself."

In the annals of complex and tortuous father-son relationships, the Dawson story stands out.

I am no stranger to father-son disputes, having experienced a decade-long falling-out with my own father over my resistance to America's involvement in the Vietnam War and the military draft that supported it. He and I remained distant from each other, each within our respective ideological fortifications. I feel a kinship: both George Mercer Dawson and I landed in the British Columbia Interior for reasons of belief. Or the lack thereof.

Turmoil, both personal and national, seems to thread through the metasequoia story. Wang Zhan the botanist spent years on the run in his own country, dodging Japanese invaders. In 1943 he joined Chiang Kai-shek's new Kuomintang government as a forester. During one of his inspection tours in the central part of the country, a bout of malaria forced him to stop and rest in a small village. There, locals told him about an unusual tree species growing in the rugged mountains nearby. Malaria was no match for Wang's botanical curiosity: after recuperating, he hiked out to see the grove, and the rest is history.

I am not altogether sure what meaning to draw from my 50-million-year personal foliage coincidence. How could I have not known that metasequoia had been rediscovered? Or that it is now grown as a landscape specimen tree? Should I marvel at the amazing durability of nature's creatures? Or the humbling of the human race by this ancient tree? Or the insignificance of my medical situation, an old man with low-grade prostate cancer, compared with the grand scheme of human conditions?

When I do the cancer walk, starting from free parking, past the metasequoia and along the five blocks to Kelowna's Sindi Ahluwalia Hawkins Cancer Centre, I am part of the unspoken fellowship. We are all heading there for either diagnosis, consultation, chemotherapy or radiation. Fellowship continues in the radiation waiting rooms, where we trade magazines, offer up our chair next to the window, or chat about many subjects except the obvious one. Our famed Canadian politeness is much in evidence here. On the coffee table in each waiting room is a massive three-thousand-piece jigsaw puzzle that takes days to complete, each patient fitting a few pieces as they wait. When the puzzle is finally finished, a staffer disassembles it and takes the box to an adjacent waiting room, and the process starts over.

As I do the walk, I am keenly aware of my trivial membership in this community, since prostate cancer is rarely fatal. As the saying goes, many men die with prostate cancer, but few die of it. My token membership is forcefully driven home to me whenever

I pass a middle-aged woman wearing the telltale headscarf. But like the metasequoia, Wang Zhan and the younger Dawson, we are unique, and we all soldier on.

6
SAGEBRUSH, SCIENCE AND SHIFTING MOSAICS

IN A CAREFULLY timed move, I swerve off the outside lane onto a narrow turnout. As I leave my car, the whine and yammer of traffic is deafening. This turnout is totally claustrophobic. On one side of me are towering silt cliffs; on the other side, four lanes of hyperactive Highway 97 traffic, and just beyond that, the riprapped shoreline of Okanagan Lake. Struggling through the dense brush beyond the turnout, I reach the mouth of a narrow, steep-sided ravine that has cut down through the silt cliff. The ravine is thickly clothed in waist-high wild ryegrass, and footing is uncertain as I climb toward my destination. The fine, silty soil of the cliff, unstable at the best of times, is slippery from a recent rain. I brought my hiking stick specifically for this adventure, and several times it plunges right down to the handle. I stay alert for sinkholes, which I know can be covered over with dead grass. The one advantage of this crazy terrain is its forgiveness: if you fall, you land on soft ground. There are no rocks, anywhere.

Five minutes into the ravine, and now silence reigns. The 120-kilometre-per-hour chaos of Highway 97, which courses through the Okanagan on its way from California to the Yukon, is forgotten. Struggling slowly upward, I review my cursory understanding of the geology of this particular place.

Start with the Late Pleistocene, say about twelve thousand years ago. The massive glacier that once filled the entire Okanagan Basin is now melting rapidly. Huge volumes of muddy meltwater rush down from the mountains above. As the silt-laden meltwater

The Sky and the Patio

reaches a much-reduced glacier at the valley bottom, it slows down, depositing its cargo against a vertical ice edge, like silt behind a modern dam. Fast-forward several millennia, while still repeating these meltwater/silt deposition events every summer. Silt continues to accrete against the glacier edge. Fast-forward again, until the valley-bottom glacier is totally gone, replaced by a lake bounded by a fifteen-storey-high vertical silt cliff, with a dead-level silt plateau behind. At some point, a minor (in geological terms) flood event perforates the silt cliff, carving out this ravine I now struggle through.

Looking closely at the exposed walls of the ravine, I see hundreds of faint horizontal bands with slight variations in silt colour and grain size, bands laid down by those same annual flood/deposition events. Curiously, the bands show absolutely no evidence of fossil vegetation. Nothing, not even dark stains from moss or algae. The end of the Pleistocene must have been quite an inhospitable time.

After forty-five minutes of criss-crossing my way up the ravine, avoiding the steepest portions and the sinkholes, I arrive at my destination: the isolated silt plateau sandwiched between mountain and lake, and covered in sagebrush.

The sage here is dense, waist-high and timeless. I am half an hour as the crow flies from my home in Summerland, yet this has the feel of genuine wilderness. I thread my way randomly, in between the shrubs. Their leaves are uniformly grey, the branches and trunks a dark ash colour. I know from counting annual growth rings that a typical sagebrush lifespan is around forty years, but here even the juvenile shrubs look ancient. The subtle but powerful sage scent speaks to me of horses and cowboys, of Nevada and Utah. Indeed, I notice piles of dung from the feral horses that roam the area. This is a landscape that painters like Charlie Russell or Will James would have felt right at home in. Or a writer like Zane Grey. Or the Sons of the Pioneers, singing "Git Along, Little Dogies."

Like the ravine's path, my reasons for hiking to this plateau are convoluted. The quest began with an archival ramble through the scientific literature on range and grassland management in British

Columbia's Southern Interior. Although scientific papers can be very opaque, they do follow a superbly rational format: Abstract, Introduction, Materials and Methods, Results, Conclusions and References. Reading this literature is like delving into genealogy: an intriguing reference cited at the end of one paper leads you to acquire and read *that* intriguing paper, which of course contains another relevant and intriguing reference to another. At one point in my daisy-chain reading, I ran across reference to *An Ecological Study of Sagebrush in Interior British Columbia*, by one L. Marchand. That name rang a bell, but more for Canadian federal politics than for rangeland research. I was unable to find the paper anywhere online, so I investigated further and found that it was actually a 1964 master's thesis from the University of Idaho. Intrigued, I contacted that university's library and found that they did have the original copy, and if I was prepared to put my grandchildren up as collateral, I could actually borrow it.

As I waited impatiently for the thesis to arrive, I gathered some biographical detail on Leonard Marchand. Born on the Okanagan Reserve near Vernon in 1933, Mr. Marchand registered a number of Indigenous "firsts" in his long and varied career: first Indigenous person to graduate from the University of British Columbia's School of Agriculture; first to receive a master's degree from the University of Idaho; first to become a federal member of Parliament, for the Kamloops-Cariboo riding, and first to become a federal cabinet member. He went on to be the third Indigenous person to be named to the Canadian Senate, after James Gladstone and Guy Williams. Along the way, Mr. Marchand became a member of the Order of Canada and the Order of British Columbia.

My dusty archival research soon led me to a real person. A colleague told me that Len Marchand lived in Kamloops. I tracked down a phone number and called him. We had a delightful chat. Toward the end of the call, I told him I was borrowing his thesis. In response he said, "You know, I loaned my copy of that thesis to a colleague years ago, and he lost it."

I decided to take action. As soon as the thesis arrived, I had it scanned, printed and bound. Shortly after, I had the pleasure of hand-delivering the resurrected thesis to Len and his lovely wife, Donna, at their Kamloops home. As we thumbed through the thesis together, I was stunned by the amount of work that had gone into it. Len's sagebrush research involved vegetation monitoring, taxonomy, soil studies, root growth studies, common garden studies and genetic analysis. The list of his BC field plot locations was also daunting: Kamloops, Summerland, Alkali Lake, Shingle Creek, Garnett Valley, Rock Creek and Anarchist Mountain, with additional sites in Squaw Butte, Oregon and Dubois, Idaho. Anyone doing that same amount of research work today would demand at least two PhDs for it!

After completing his thesis, Len was all set to do a doctorate in range management, but Canadian politics intervened. As a youngster, Len had met George Manuel, head of the North American Indian Brotherhood, and the two stayed in touch. Manuel had long advocated for an Indigenous presence in Canadian federal politics, and saw Marchand as the ideal candidate for such a role. In 1965, Manuel convinced the minister of citizenship and immigration (Indian Affairs was under that ministry at the time) to name Len as special assistant, and the rest is history.

In 2000, Len published his autobiography, *Breaking Trail*. It is a fascinating read.

Len Marchand passed on in 2016, at the age of 83. When I heard that news, I resolved to visit his Summerland research site as a means of paying my respects. His thesis gave a pretty clear description of the plot location, and there was a picture as well. Len would have accessed the site by way of the Summerland Research Station, just to the north. That option was not available to me, due to locked gates and security fences around the station. Thus the ravine, accessed by the narrow turnout off Highway 97.

There was serious intent behind my random, zigzag walk on this sagebrush flat: I was on the lookout for Len's plot stakes, and sure enough, I found a few. Some were round like broom handles, others were lath strips, but all were weathered and broken, probably by horse hooves. Then I stumbled upon a metal marker, about a metre long, with a sharpened end and a red-painted ring at the top. It was the same plot marker that was evident in the 1964 site photo in Len's thesis. I did a little victory dance, likely the first ever on that lonesome sagebrush flat.

My adventure was beginning to feel a bit like the archaeology of rangeland science, or even deeper, a dive into the elective affinities of a prominent Canadian. Those weathered shards of plot stakes were tangible markers of Marchand's very intimate relationship with a natural ecosystem. Len had delved deep into the inner mechanics of sagebrush, at a dozen far-flung locations. He analyzed leaf shape variation. He studied their root growth in specially designed growth chambers. He tested the fluorescence of their seeds, and the growth rate of their seedlings. He was among the first to recognize that British Columbia hosted three different but closely related sage types. The classic Wyoming big sage (*Artemisia tridentata v. tridentata*) is dominant in many parts of the western United States, and extends into BC's dry valleys, all the way up to the junction of the Fraser and Chilcotin rivers. Southern Alberta also has a few scattered big sage communities. Vasey's sage (*A. tridentata v. vaseyana*) is found only at high elevations in BC's South Okanagan–Similkameen. Threetip sage (*A. tripartita*) is found only at low elevations in the same area. Extending the sage saga, there is a fourth one in the BC Interior: pasture sage (*Artemisia frigida*), a low-growing type lacking the upright, gnarly stems of its cousins. Pasture sage is found throughout the BC Interior and even up into the Yukon. This plant is the one traditionally used by First Nations for smudging.

To round out the sage story, there is a raft of other forb (as opposed to shrub) Artemisias — the mugworts, the sageworts and the wormwoods: most are native, a few are introduced weeds. Not only are the Artemisias a taxonomist's nightmare, they are often confused with the Salvia genus, which includes culinary sage. Even though they are totally different plants, the Artemisia sages and the Salvia sages give off a similar odour. The Utah sage that Zane Grey's *Riders of the Purple Sage* passed through was actually a Salvia.

Edwin Tisdale was the godfather of rangeland research in British Columbia, and he determined the direction of Len Marchand's early career. When the Federal Agriculture Research Station at Kamloops opened in 1935, Tisdale was named chief botanist. Right away, Tisdale developed a research interest in the sagebrush question, establishing research plots at Tranquille, near the Tuberculosis Sanatorium. In 1947, Tisdale moved on to become a professor of range science at the University of Idaho, but his legacy at the Kamloops station lived on. In 1960, as a first-year university student, Len took a summer job at the station. He in turn was motivated by research into sagebrush. After a summer there: "I applied for educational leave and enrolled in a master's program at the University of Idaho, where I could study under Ed Tisdale, a Canadian who had earned a solid reputation in my area of interest. Much of his early work had been done at the Kamloops station, so he was the perfect advisor for my master's thesis, which I determined would be an ecological study of sagebrush in BC."

So it is not surprising that one of Len's many sagebrush research plots was in the same Tranquille location as Tisdale's, some twenty-five years later.

I have had the privilege of exploring the landscapes of Tranquille and adjacent Lac du Bois, a lovely and fascinating complex of ecosystems just across the Thompson River from Kamloops. Beginning at river level at Tranquille (350 metres above sea level) and extending gradually northward to Opax Hill at 1,400 metres, the area is an open, south-facing textbook of BC Interior vegetation zones, from sagebrush all the way up to spruce. Research plots and grazing exclosures, both old and new, some forgotten and some active, are found everywhere in Lac du Bois. One of the perennial research questions here — and elsewhere — is the current and historical role of sagebrush.

Sagebrush has three distinctive qualities. It is incredibly drought-tolerant; cows and wild mammals refuse to eat it; and it is extremely flammable, due to the volatile oils contained in its leaves. Applying a lighted drip torch to the base of a mature sagebrush is always a startling event: there is a loud thump as bright orange flames instantly engulf the entire plant. Five seconds later the fire is out, leaving bare, blackened branches and a thin scattering of white ash on the ground. Very occasionally, one sees subsequent sprouting around the base, but generally sagebrush shrubs are totally killed by fire. Because they are fairly short-lived and easily fire-killed, sagebrush does not offer us the historical fire record that fire-scarred trees provide, so we must rely on other means of inference. One fragment of sagebrush historical information comes from the Reverend George Monro Grant, who passed through Kamloops in the fall of 1872. He described the local vegetation this way:

> ...the total absence of underbrush and the dry grey grass everywhere covering the ground....The only timber in the district is a knotty red pine [ponderosa], and as the trees grow widely apart, and the bunchgrass underneath is clean, unmixed with weeds and shrubs, and uniform in color, the country has a well-kept parklike appearance....

Much of lower Tranquille and Lac du Bois, and other parts of BC's Southern Interior, are now clogged with the same dense, waist-high Wyoming big sage that I see on the Summerland plateau. So the question arises: what is the historical role of sagebrush in these dry ecosystems? The answer hinges on three natural disturbances: fire, grazing and drought. Fire reduces or eliminates sagebrush cover. Grazing encourages it, by weakening the palatable grasses and forbs, giving a competitive advantage to totally inedible sagebrush. Drought encourages sagebrush in the same way, by weakening the less deep-rooted grasses and forbs. But there is a caveat: periods of drought are often associated with greater fire frequency. However, this caveat must be paired with another one: sagebrush is a prolific seed producer, and recently burned areas can often host a carpet of new sage seedlings.

Rummaging through early archival photos of BC certainly confirms Grant's observations, that the density of sagebrush in our dry valleys was far less then than it is now. First Nations did cultural burns in dry forest areas, but they also burned sagebrush grasslands. Their burning practices enhanced forage for deer, sheep, mountain goats and elk, as well as for — more recently — horses. Their burns also encouraged various food and medicinal plants, and reduced tick populations that would otherwise plague human and beast alike. The creation of reserves in the 1860s and the brutal suppression of First Nation traditional practices put an abrupt end to cultural burning. This, coupled with cattle grazing and the advent of total fire suppression beginning in the 1940s, synergized to produce the sagebrush-dominated stands we see today.

This does not imply that sagebrush was rare or non-existent in pre-European-contact times. A good way to visualize our pre-contact dry ecosystems is as a shifting mosaic. Imagine patches of just burned, recently burned, long-ago burned — and every stage in between — shifting over time and geography.

Parts of the Okanagan Indian Reserve, where Len Marchand spent his childhood, are rank with big sagebrush. As a child he rode around the reserve on horseback with his grandfather, so he would have heard many stories from him, as well as from his grandmother, an expert in traditional plant medicines. Based on those childhood associations, Len would have been well aware of First Nation cultural burning practices. That knowledge may have lain quietly in his personal background as he selected sagebrush as his research topic. Len Marchand helped to lay the groundwork for the emerging interplay between Indigenous ecological knowledge and western science.

Finishing my exploration of Len's plateau, I reluctantly head toward the ravine and home. Just before I leave the sagebrush-covered expanse, I turn back for a last look. It seems timeless, but I know that to be a comfortable, romantic illusion. I must redefine my sense of timelessness so that I experience it as an endlessly shifting mosaic, while still retaining the romance. This sagebrush plateau combines the scientific, the honorary and the romantic. Hard to access, but well worth it.

7
COMPOST FETISHISM AND THE DIRTY DOZEN

OUR TOWN'S WASTE collection service provides us with three sturdy plastic bins, one for garbage, one for recycling and one for "yard waste." I consider this last a grievous ecological and personal insult. Organic materials from gardens and landscaping are certainly not "waste," and furthermore, what are my neighbours thinking, dragging their monthly bin to the curb chock full of lovely future soil organic material, which they have produced right in their own yard, only to give away? I have to give our town credit, though; it has a large-scale recycling operation where yard waste is mixed with biosolids from the sewage treatment plant, and the resulting compost is sold at a very reasonable price. This option is fine for some people, but not for me. Gollum-like, I hoard My Precious, my non-edible yard, vineyard and garden output. The yard waste bins the town provides to us are wheeled, have a hinged green lid and are quite sturdy. I have repurposed mine as a compost bin, to supplement my ongoing lawn, garden, vineyard and landscaping experiments. In the spring the bin receives suitable prunings; over the summer it gets dandelion corpses and lawn clippings; in the fall it gets tree leaves, plus the lees from my wine-grape pressings; in the winter it gets ash from the wood stove; and year-round it gets the kitchen scraps. And I do not hesitate to piss in the bin as the occasion arises. Then, the next spring, I remove and spread a winter's worth of lovely, aromatic compost, and start the cycle over again.

The Sky and the Patio

My greed for compost is greater than a single yard can supply, so I have ventured farther afield, foraging for raw materials. Our local chain coffee shop produces endless free bags of spent coffee grounds, so I regularly add these to my compost mix. Coffee grounds are neutral to slightly acidic, so they not only provide organic matter, but also help to moderate the slight alkalinity of my Okanagan soil. During the sweet corn season, grocery stores offer a surprise bounty. For some unexplained reason, shoppers prefer shucking their corn purchases right in the store instead of doing it at home. So great hulking bags of eminently compostable corn shuck are often available for the asking. My composting effort provides me with some penance for all the reams of unwanted but unavoidable consumer plastic packaging that arrive in our household.

One of the dilemmas of growing backyard fruit trees is they tend to produce more than you can use. Or the fruit gets buggy because you haven't sprayed. Either way, we can honour the excess bounty these apple, cherry, pear and apricot trees produce by giving the good stuff to the food bank and then composting the rest.

The little stainless-steel scrap bucket on our kitchen counter is another key source of raw materials. Broccoli bums, stale bread, carrot tops, onion skins and, of course, more coffee grounds go into the bucket. A layer of high-powered, wet materials like these needs to be balanced off in the compost bin with another layer of dry, fibrous stuff. Two big Norway maples in the front yard stand at the ready, providing copious amounts of fallen leaves. Before composting them, I rake the leaves into a big pile and run my electric lawnmower over the pile many times until most are reduced to small flakes. My eyeball ratio of kitchen scraps (high nitrogen, low carbon) to maple leaves (high carbon, low nitrogen) is a very crude attempt to hit the ideal carbon-to-nitrogen composting ratio, which is 20:1. If I were to measure this, it might mean forty leaves for each broccoli bum, but I'm not about to get that precise. There are many other parameters for ideal composting: moisture 50–65 percent, pH 5.5–8.0, oxygen level 5–10 percent, temperature between 40 and 60 degrees centigrade. In an effort to speed up the composting process, I repurposed a small solar panel and mounted it above the bin. Then I connected it to a twelve-volt heating element and buried that in the centre of the bin. Now I visualize hordes of happy little microbes gathered around the element, munching and basking in the sun's transformed glory, even when outside temperatures are in the minus range.

The solar technology addition was fun but unnecessary. Backyard composting is very forgiving; it rewards casualness and imprecision. If you keep it moist but not wet, turn it periodically and wait long enough, you get product. Product unique to your yard, and to your idiosyncrasies.

The paradox of compost bins, just like woodpiles, is that the good stuff is always at the bottom. So I have a second bin, of my own purchase, and I periodically rotate the contents from one to the other. This process requires an ancient and venerable tool that I am proud to own two of: the pitchfork.

Good, well-aged compost has an unmistakable and pleasant bouquet. If it hasn't aged long enough or is too dry, there is no bouquet. If it has stayed too wet, there will be a rank, rotten-egg odour. Along with the pitchfork, a good nose is a handy composting accessory.

Taking the time to put four carrot tops into a compost bucket is of course meaningless, unless you keep on doing it for a decade. Composting evokes the long curve of ecological time, and the accretion of small but daily acts. Humans have always been conservers and recyclers at heart, and during this rapidly collapsing episode of the consumer society, composting helps us get back to those roots.

Plant nutrients are easy enough to come by. The great benefit of compost is not as a nutrient supplier, but as raw material for stable organic matter, that invisible, ignored and hugely important component of soils. Organic matter binds with soil particles, creating a matrix that retains water, aerates the soil mass, provides habitat for microbiota, and retains and slowly releases nutrients. If soil were compared to human anatomy, organic matter would be the blood.

The science of soils — pedology — is an obscure but fascinating profession, one that reaches out to plant science on the upper end and to geology on the lower. It has its own language, which borrows heavily from the Russian, as well as its own neologisms, like *podsol* and *slickenside*. Pedologists are by and large interesting folks, more comfortable with the humanities than people in other hard sciences. A typical soil science conference will have a few talks involving the history, the poetry or even the psychology of soil.

Soil science lives and dies by horizons, those maddeningly indistinct layers composed of slightly different textures, colours and chemistries. A typical soil will have five horizons of varying thickness. The Soils of Canada Glossary lists some two hundred and fifty different horizon types, each of course with its own abbreviation. A field day with a group of soil scientists consists of a few minutes of shovel work to dig a soil pit, followed by lengthy and esoteric discussions leading to (not always consensual) definitions of the soil's various horizons. For those of us who discover fairly dramatic soil changes just from our backyard to our front yard, we should offer sympathy to these hard-working folks who attempt to classify soils on a regional, national or even international basis.

Drilling down into our own backyard's pedological parameters, I know from hard experience that we are perched on a glaciofluvial terrace, with uncounted billions of rounded and tightly packed rocks lying in wait a few centimetres below the surface. To delve further, I consulted a 1994 soil survey map of the Okanagan and discovered that our yard lies in the Dartmouth Soil Series. In the Canadian Soil Classification System, "series" is the lowest level, sort of equivalent to "species" on the natural history side. Curious, I attempted to move upward in the classification hierarchy from "series" to "family" to "subgroup" to "great group" to "order," but got lost along the way. Fortunately, I found another document that identified Dartmouth as a member of the Orthic great group and of the Chernozemic order, the soils of dry grasslands.

The soil survey map identified a number of Dartmouth polygons up and down the Okanagan Valley. Surprisingly, our polygon was only the size of about six city blocks, indicating the very fine scale of the mapping effort. According to the survey, the Dartmouth Series is categorized as dark brown, with a texture of silt loam, a slightly alkaline pH and 39 percent by volume of "coarse fragments" (a polite soils euphemism for rocks). The most significant statistic for me was this: Dartmouth's soil organic matter percentage is extremely low: 2.7 percent. For comparison, the best untilled grassland soils of the Canadian Prairies have up to 12 percent organic matter, and peat bog soils can have over 60 percent.

Soil scientists put great stock in colour, which is largely driven by organic matter content. Just like painters and interior designers, the soils folk break colour down into hue, value and chroma. In fact, one of the pioneers of soil science, Hans Jenny (1899–1992), spent the twilight of his long career studying the images of soil in classical and contemporary landscape paintings. There is even a technique of painting that uses various finely ground soils in lieu of paints. The technique recaptures the subdued and finely gradated colours seen in Renaissance landscape paintings.

In general, the more organic matter there is in the soil, the darker it is. Think of sand at one extreme and peat at the other. Whether a soil is classified as brown, dark brown or black is largely dependent on organic matter content. Following this logic, I wondered if my years of composting and mulching our yard might have actually changed its classification. Rooting through my office file boxes, I finally found my pocket-sized *Soil Color Chart*. Named after the art educator Albert Munsell (1858–1918), it has an extensive series of colour swatches that range from light grey through yellow, light brown and dark brown and all the way to black. Each swatch has a pea-sized viewing hole next to it. I took a random spadeful of soil from our yard and held it directly under the colour chart, with the sun behind me, as per Mr. Munsell's instructions. Roving through the various colours, the closest match turned out to be "very dark brown," one shade away from "black," which pleased me no end. Now I am motivated to pay for an actual soil test, to see if my composting allows me to graduate from Dartmouth to a new, backyard series, which I will either name as "Gayton," or possibly "Yippee Calle," after the name of my vest-pocket vineyard.

Much of traditional soil science has been focused simply on facilitating the delivery of the agronomic Big Three: nitrogen, phosphorous and potassium. But recently organic matter has gained considerable attention. Soil organic matter is now being actively investigated as a low-tech mechanism for carbon sequestration: the capture and long-term storage of atmospheric carbon.

Our monthly Yard Waste Wednesdays always catch me by surprise, when I see all those green-lidded bins lined up on our residential street. Instinctively, my mind turns to thoughts of petty theft. Most people put their bins out in the morning, but a few put them out the night before, which would provide me with the cover of darkness. But then pragmatism intervenes. I couldn't actually steal the bins themselves, so what would I load the loot into, and how much noise would it make? Surely dogs would start barking, neighbours would awaken and there would be bad press if I was caught. Our weekly paper would no doubt print some lurid headline, like "Deranged Senior Loots Yard Waste Bins."

As I dole out compost from my wheelbarrow, I pass by the bluebunch wheatgrasses I have planted. One of the many features of this tall, stately native bunchgrass and its cousins the fescues is a remarkable root network composed of hundreds of hair-like, fibrous roots. They do explore deeply: I have dug grassland soil pits and found bluebunch roots a metre and more down into the soil profile. These roots die continuously and are replaced continuously. Within three or four years, the entire root mass — twice the weight of the above-ground parts — will have replaced itself. Those tiny, hair-like root corpses are quickly converted to organic matter, creating the rich Chernozemic grassland soils that are prized for dryland agriculture throughout the world.

There is another emergent principle of our native bunchgrasses — bluebunch, plus rough fescue, Idaho fescue and a few others: the carbon-rich organic matter they deposit in the soil is relatively permanent, and cheap. The only expense we incur turning native grasslands into extensive carbon sinks is ensuring the preservation and health of those grasslands.

My yard's native plants — bluebunch, fescue, antelopebrush, saskatoon, ponderosa pine and a number of other plants I am inordinately fond of — never get compost. This seems very discriminatory until one considers the habitat Okanagan native plants evolved in: dry climate and generally poor soils. In general, these upland native plants are tough, slow growing and slow to reproduce. They are accustomed to dry, low-nutrient and low-organic-matter soil environments. Reversing those conditions doesn't necessarily favour them, and in fact tends to favour weeds. These invasives thrive on excess nitrogen and water, and can colonize and reproduce at blinding speed. Rich, recently disturbed soils are nirvana for invasives. Over my years of relentless weeding, I have developed one rule and one axiom. The rule: never bend over to pull just one weed. The axiom: the more time you have, the more weeds there are.

Bonded as I am to grasslands, I am attempting to create a Southern Interior grassland microcosm in a tiny portion of our yard, about the size of two ping-pong tables. This garden is, in essence, a miniature ecological restoration, since our yard would have been native grassland prior to European settlement. This re-creation has become an end in itself, a self-imposed test of patience, perseverance and the willingness to accept very limited success. I have been reasonably successful with grassland shrubs (antelopebrush, sagebrush, saskatoon, Oregon grape) and less so with the big bunchgrasses (bluebunch wheatgrass, rough fescue, sand dropseed). But the native flowers have been the biggest challenge. The gorgeous spring-blooming arrowleaf balsamroot, found everywhere in the grasslands of the Okanagan-Similkameen, is damnably hard to grow. Even very accomplished native plant gardeners shake their heads as they recount failure after failure to establish this plant, with its delightful yellow pop-art flowers.

In contrast, I have been tremendously successful with grassland weeds. My native plant plot hosts a rogue's gallery of them. Cheatgrass, bulbous bluegrass, quackgrass, yellow salsify, storksbill, shining geranium, dandelion, morning glory, pineapple weed, black medic, tumble mustard — I could go on. This is my list, but gardeners in every ecological region and subregion would have their own particular Dirty Dozen. Cheatgrass is perhaps my biggest curse. Widespread through the dry grasslands of Western North America, the annual cheatgrass was first identified in BC by John Macoun in the 1880s. Indigenous peoples on the Canadian Prairies referred to the grass as "white man's foot," since as soon as soon as settlers appeared, so did the grass. This damnable annual can act like an internal parasite of my big native bunchgrasses, somehow able to establish and grow right in the centre of a dense, healthy clump. Cheatgrass is native to a huge swath of the planet: Europe, North Africa and Southwest Asia. That certainly speaks to its ability to adapt to different habitats.

Weeding in a native grassland garden is problematic. In spring, all grasses look pretty much the same, whether they are native or introduced. Identification at this stage requires very close inspection of leaf structure, colour and hairiness, challenging when one is standing upright with weeding tool in hand. I have had to resort to a kind of probabilistic grass weeding, assuming I make a correct identification about seventy-five percent of the time. As I do this, I am always reminded of Henry David Thoreau's resonant phrase "making invidious distinctions with his hoe."

Our rainbarrel drains slowly into a low spot in the yard, where I was able to establish the wonderfully pungent native sweetgrass (*Hierochloe odorata*). Over the years, however, it has been gradually overwhelmed by quackgrass and Kentucky bluegrass. I have had better luck with basin wildrye (*Leymus cinereus*), a tall, stately native grass found in various parts of the Southern Interior. It is not a true wetland species like sweetgrass, but it does favour draws and depressions where it can access subsurface moisture.

The spaces between the native shrubs and the big bunchgrasses are my real challenge. In nature, these spaces have a diverse mosaic of various small forbs, grasses and lichens that mature by early summer and then go dormant. To replicate this mosaic in my native plant garden would require a full-on botanical assault: identification, seed collection, greenhouse plant propagation, soil testing and water requirement analysis. Short of that, I content myself with keeping down the weeds and hoping the odd native forb might emerge from the chaos. The American nature writer Stephanie Mills says ecological restoration is not about control, but surrender. I think I understand what she means in a philosophical sense, but not when it comes to cheatgrass.

There are other native plants in our yard, beyond the two-ping-pong-table reserve. I like the eclecticism in mixing natives, near-natives and domestics. A wolf willow next to a bed of geraniums, or a bleeding heart sheltered by an antelopebrush.

I have never used herbicides in my yard, but I do have a useful alternative, in the form of ten percent cleaning vinegar, which I use as an organic contact herbicide. It is cheap, and I go through several jugs of it every spring. Before I apply it, I wait for a series of two or three warm, dry days, so the weeds are a bit water-stressed. Getting up in the morning, I check the weather report; if there is no rain in the forecast for that day, then I am in go mode. I pour a jug of vinegar into a pan on the stove and heat it up to bathtub temperature to increase its potency, then pour it into my backpack sprayer and patrol the yard, paying close attention to edges along fences, sidewalks and driveway. The vinegar treatment seems to work quite well on weeds that have lush, flat-lying leaves, like dandelion or shining geranium. The acid dissolves the waxy coating on the leaves, opening the plant up to death by dehydration. The beauty of vinegar (acetic acid) is its profoundly simple molecular structure, CH_3COOH. That means it is quickly broken down by soil microbiota, leaving no residual effect.

Resisting the impulse to water and fertilize is just one of the challenges of native plant gardening. Even though I have become very strict, I see the native shrubs in my garden adopting a different growth form than they display in nature. In spite of restricting water, fertilizer and compost, I distort their growth forms by creating an environment that is too favourable. In the wild, these species tend to grow upright, compact and stiff; in the garden, they are typically lanky, floppy and low-growing, and thus much more susceptible

The Sky and the Patio

to winter snowpress. My spring pruning activity tries to address this by cutting off the lower and outward-spreading branches of the native shrubs. These include saskatoon, sagebrush, antelopebrush, sticky currant, Oregon grape and rabbitbrush.

These last two species, Oregon grape (*Mahonia aquifolium*) and rabbitbrush (*Ericameria nauseosa*), are part of a triumvirate that includes snowbrush (*Ceanothus velutinus*). A colleague of mine who specializes in native pollinator bees tells me that by encouraging these three shrubs in my yard, I provide forage for dozens of different native bee species. Oregon grape and rabbitbrush are very easy to grow; the lovely, evergreen-leaved snowbrush is heartbreakingly difficult. I have attempted several transplants and failed each time. I keep asking myself, "If this plant can happily grow on some bony, highly disturbed roadcut, why not in my garden?"

Walking our Okanagan grasslands, a soils paradox is apparent: invasive plants are everywhere until you cross into a dry, bony spot with poor soils. There, you find a delightful assortment of tiny natives and virtually no weeds. These pockets send an obvious but counterintuitive message to the neophyte native-plant gardener: be sparing with water and fertilizer, and be patient.

Hopefully, the two-ping-pong-table section will someday be strictly native plants, but the rest of the yard is a mix of native and introduced grasses, forbs, shrubs and trees. A fan of diversity, I call this Landscape Eclecticism, even though the mix is mostly by accident rather than by design.

As I plan my spring composting application from the comfort of the patio, I will be gifting some plants and scrupulously ignoring others. And I do thank the soil scientists who continue to unravel the immense complexity of their chosen material. To those humble and persistent men and women, I raise my dirty glass, smudged here and there with fingerprints of Dartmouth.

8
COWBOY DREAMS

IT WAS EARLY afternoon when I reached the national park. After many hours on Saskatchewan back roads, it was good to get out, stretch my legs and start on to the interpretive trail. The Frenchman River was not far off, and 70 Mile Butte was visible in the distance. The solitude and spectacular ecology of this Grasslands National Park make it a haven for seekers, romantics and avoiders of the beaten tourist track. Because it is located in the far southwestern corner of the province, hard by the Montana border, few visitors arrive here on a whim.

I was a minor participant in the contentious early park-planning meetings of the 1980s, and the purpose of this road trip to Saskatchewan was to visit this now-protected national treasure. I was only on the trail for a few minutes when I realized all human sign had vanished — no buildings, no power lines, not even a fence post. Just this humble sojourner on an eternal grassland.

Walking on, I began to feel a sense of déjà vu, not of my previous trips here, but of something else. What was it about these subdued pastels of grass, of rimrock and badland, of the endless vistas under the massive dome of Prairie sky, that made them so familiar?

That night, settled into Val Marie's motel, I pulled out my well-worn copy of Wallace Stegner's *Wolf Willow*, which I had purposely brought on this trip. The book is a memoir of Stegner's childhood life in the nearby town of Eastend, and is essential reading for any southwest Saskatchewan traveller. As I thumbed through the pages, this bookmarked passage stood out:

The Sky and the Patio

> Lying on a hillside where I once sprawled among the crocuses, watching the town herd and snaring May's emerging gophers, I feel how the world still reduces me to a point, and then measures itself from me. Perhaps the meadowlark singing from a fencepost — a meadowlark whose dialect I recognize — feels the same way. All points on the circumference are equidistant from him; in him all radii begin; all diameters run through him; if he moves, a new geometry creates itself around him. No wonder he sings. It is a good country that can make anyone feel so.

In spite of that resonant passage, some lingering sense of familiarity still nagged at me. The next morning, after a late breakfast at the local café, I decided to tour Val Marie's small museum. There, hanging on the wall, was my déjà vu resolution: a reproduction of a painting by the American cowboy artist and writer Will James. *Line Camp* is the painting's title, and it depicts a rough log cabin with a sod roof. In the early days of prairie ranching, cattle were moved long distances, and rough cabins (line camps) were placed at strategic locations for cowboys to overnight along the trail. In this painting, smoke issues from the cabin's stovepipe, the front door is open, and a saddled horse stands in front of the cabin. A rope runs from the horse's bridle along the ground and in through the cabin's open door. The painting tells a mute story; horse and rider are closely bonded, and the horse is waiting for his cowboy to finish breakfast so the two of them can start the day's work.

The painting's horse and cabin subjects are compelling and finely rendered, but what really drew me in were the subtle colorations of grass and sky, of the shallow river valley behind, and of the bare rimrock in the distance. I knew that painting. From my childhood.

As a kid, I wanted to be a cowboy. That seems desperately old-fashioned now, but as a suburban American adolescent in the 1950s, I yearned for that simple and passionate life. Riding rimrock country on a trusted horse, through sagebrush and arroyo, with chaps and lariat, minding cattle on the range. While my contemporaries built youthful fantasies around Superman and GI Joe, mine were drawn from my father's bookshelf, where I found western novels, including those of Will James.

Immensely popular from the late 1920s to the early 1940s, James was a folk hero to my father's generation. He was not an author who chanced to write about cowboys; instead, he cowboyed, and then wrote about it. And painted it. His heartland was the western open range, and his twenty-six novels contain glorious sketches and paintings of wild mustangs, lone horsemen, bronc riders and sagebrush. I took a deep adolescent dive into his book *Smoky the Cowhorse*, which was published in 1926 and included colour reproductions of *Line Camp* and several other paintings.

Will James was, in every way, the quintessential American cowboy, but the director of the Val Marie museum revealed his hidden Canadian backstory. Upon my return home, I did some research: Will James was actually Ernest Dufault, born in Saint-Nazaire-d'Acton, in the province of Quebec, in 1892.

Like me, the young Ernest was also smitten by stories of cowboys, and he spent all his spare time dreaming about and sketching imagined life in the West. Leaving his Quebec home at the tender age of fifteen, he got off the train in Saskatchewan and began working on cattle ranches in the southwest country. His learning curve was enormous: within two years, the young Ernest had mastered English, horseback riding and cowpunching. And he continued to sketch, on envelopes, bunkhouse walls, on anything else he could lay his hands on. Horses dominated his art, and that love affair continued for all of his short life.

Slowly, young Dufault began to create his own western image, both on sketch paper and in his own mind; ten-gallon hat, black vest, scarf knotted around the neck, roachkiller cowboy boots, pant cuffs turned up, a Bull Durham roll-your-own held casually in the side of his mouth. Always mounted on a horse, or standing next to one. With jet-black hair, hawk nose and chiselled features, this young man was as handsome in real life as he was in his many self-portraits.

Name has much to do with image, and during this time Ernest began experimenting with Anglo, western-sounding handles for himself, eventually settling on the monosyllabic Will James. That was perhaps a prophetic early step along a journey toward fame, fortune and an untimely death.

As I researched further, I found references to Ernest Dufault/ Will James popping up in various Prairie communities during his six-year stay in Western Canada. One of his trademarks was to leave a signed and dated sketch or photograph of himself wherever he went. These artifacts, together with local histories and rancher accounts, have him passing through or working in communities like Maple Creek, Ravenscrag, and Gull Lake, as well as Val Marie. A sole postcard the young man sent to his family was postmarked at Sage Creek, in the isolated Milk River country of southern Alberta.

As he drifted from one ranch to another, Ernest found an older mentor in Pierre Beaupre, a fellow Québécois, who helped him learn English and the ways of the western cowboy. In 1911, they filed adjacent homestead claims in what would eventually become Grasslands National Park, nearly a century later. "Bopy," as Will affectionately called him, was to become a seminal figure in James's fictional autobiography, *Lone Cowboy*.

A scrape with the law followed by a stint in the Maple Creek jail nourished James's fugitive tendencies. Upon release, he fled south to Montana, leaving literally everything behind — his homestead claim, his partner, his family ties, his real name and his Canadian identity. Still in his twenties, he was now fully remade as Will James, Montana cowpuncher, rodeo rider, storyteller and itinerant artist. Legend has it that James met the great cowboy painter Charles M. Russell, who encouraged him in his work and got him started writing his stories down. Those early works came to the attention of the popular New York magazine *Sunset,* and soon eastern readers were devouring James's short stories and sketches.

Will James literally embraced the American West, cowboying and rodeoing through Montana, Utah and Nevada, working as a stunt rider in Hollywood, sketching, and writing everything down.

He saw himself as indestructible, but bronc riding and a habit of binge drinking were taking their toll. His marriage to Alice Conradt, daughter of a wealthy Nevada ranching family, brought some temporary stability to his life, and his stories lengthened into novels. These were wildly successful: *Smoky, Lone Cowboy* and several other books were bestsellers, reprinted over and over again.

All the James books are written in a slangy western vernacular which now seems dated and a bit silly, but which captivated readers at the time. They held particular appeal for boys, and my father admitted to being under the James spell as an adolescent, just as I was. This speaks to the power of myth, as it passes unchanged from one generation to the next.

America in the 1930s was a nation undergoing rapid urbanization and industrialization, but Will James's novels reflect none of that. His books were about frontier: there were no references to cities, factories or even automobiles, and that was part of the secret of their success. In spite of its passionate embrace of the Machine Age, American male identity was still rooted in the rugged, independent frontier cowboy, and James reinforced that belief. Writing about an unfenced, free-range ranching lifestyle that was largely gone, Will James gave factory workers, straphangers, intellectuals and adolescents alike the opportunity to fantasize that dead era back to life.

Lone Cowboy, James's "autobiography," is a fascinating fabrication. In it, he makes no mention of his Quebec roots, offering instead this fantasy origin: he is born on a remote Montana cattle ranch, and both of his parents are killed in an accident when he is a child. He is subsequently adopted and raised by the French-Canadian cowhand Bopy. Later on, Bopy drowns in an ice-filled Montana river. This clever fabrication provides a logical explanation for Will's lifelong French accent, while at the same time eliminating any possibility of story verification. All possible loose personal ends in *Lone Cowboy* have been carefully snipped off.

Will's new-found celebrity status was both a blessing and a curse. Book royalties allowed him to buy a Montana cattle ranch

The Sky and the Patio

that became a romantic haven for him and his wife, Alice. He landed movie contracts for both *Smoky* and *Lone Cowboy,* but was soon shut out of any significant role in either film because of his drinking habits. With fame came increased scrutiny, and people began to question the gaps and inconsistencies in Will's life story. Like his famous contemporary Grey Owl (real name Archie Belaney), he lived an elaborate lie. The resulting psychological pressure was enormous. Paranoid about having his real origins discovered, James swore his Quebec family to absolute secrecy, and then cut all ties with them. Not even his wife knew the true story. An obvious outlet for this anxiety was alcohol, which his celebrity status provided him with in abundance. Will's drinking binges and blackouts became more and more common, and his artistic output finally ceased altogether. When he died at age fifty of cirrhosis of the liver, the world lost a mythic — and tragic — hero.

I still have my father's copy of *Smoky*, which was given to him by his aunt in 1929, when he was eleven. The book occupies a proud place on my bookshelf, and a reprint of *Line Camp* hangs on the wall. Both serve to remind me of our mutual adolescent dream of being a cowboy. In my twenties, I did work on cattle ranches for a few years, but as a hired man, not a cowboy. My very unromantic cycle of ranch duties was mostly changing irrigation sprinklers, bucking hay and fixing fence. On rare and glorious occasions, I got to move cattle on horseback. Even though I never became a full-on cowboy, my life has been somehow tied to grass and grazer, soil and sagebrush, badland and butte. Will James had something to do with that.

That visit to Grasslands National Park will likely be my last, so I hold tight to the memories. One in particular is of a rubbing stone. A lone glacial erratic, it stands by itself in treeless, rolling prairie. Three narrow trails converge on it, from different directions, worn deeply by generations of bison. A mute landmark that speaks volumes. Another memory is a poem from Thelma Poirier, who participated in the initial hearings about the proposed park.

As a local rancher as well as a lover of prairie grasslands, she was conflicted, but ultimately sided with the park:

> reasons
> because the grama grass has not been plowed
> the buckbrush burned
> because the antelope tenders its young
> in the far ravine
> because the burrowing owl nests
> on the barren ridge
> because the rattlesnake sleeps
> undisturbed in its den
> because the sage hen struts
> first morning light
> because the golden eagle circles the far butte
> the ferruginous hawk the nearer one
> because the badger slides through the prairie wool
> invisible
> because the stones are riddled with lichen
> tapestries unturned
> because, a park

What a comfort it is to have both literary and artistic reminders of those austere and magical grasslands, in the form of *Wolf Willow*, *Line Camp* and Thelma Poirier's book of poetry, *Grasslands*.

9
A PAEAN TO THE SOCKEYE

A FAVOURITE SUMMER patio meal is a couple of slices of local bakery bread, a salad, an inexpensive but well-constructed Okanagan Chardonnay and pan-seared sockeye salmon. Our local grocery store chain owns a fleet of West Coast fishing boats, so fillets of this magnificent and accomplished fish are usually in good supply. I am too amateur to attempt the complex art of salmon barbecuing, so I focus my efforts on the kitchen stove.

Frying fillets right out of the fridge offers decent results, but marinating them first adds a whole new creative dimension. I've tried teriyaki sauce, fish sauce, Dijon mustard, Tabasco and other ingredients, but I always return to my favourite marinade, a concoction of soy sauce, lemon juice and Quebec maple syrup. This latter ingredient hints of another favourite: candied salmon. The fillet goes into a suction-top container containing my marinade mix and sits in the fridge for a few hours. During the wait, I envision the lowered atmospheric pressure slowly drawing the marinade into the gorgeous brick-red flesh of the sockeye. When I am ready to cook, I choose a frying pan with a base slightly smaller than the fillets themselves, and heat it up until the olive oil starts to smoke. Add a pat of butter, quickly mix it with the hot oil, and drop in the fillet. The noisy, messy, sizzling magic begins, and the stovetop around the pan receives a fine spray of hot oil. I have a glass pot lid at the ready, which fits snugly over the pan. When the spray threatens to go critical, I put the lid on, but only for brief periods, since it changes the cooking process from frying to steaming.

The Sky and the Patio

The accepted wisdom for salmon cooking time is ten minutes per inch of flesh, measured at the thickest part. The fillets I get are typically about half or three-quarters of an inch thick, so that takes traditional cook time down to five to seven minutes. With high heat, I ramp that down further to about two minutes on the first side, and then another minute or so on the second side. Now for the great culinary debate: start frying skin-side up, or skin-side down? A colleague showed me how to start skin-side down and then, with the aid of a razor-sharp spatula and some surgical dexterity, separate and flip the meat, leaving the skin on the pan. The double fry makes the skin delightfully crispy, like a kind of North Pacific bacon. I don't always manage this delicate separation of skin from flesh, but when I do, a culinary fist pump is in order.

When the meal is done and fillets, skin and syrup are consumed, I extend my patio time by leisurely scraping off the carbonized bits of flesh in the pan with my thumbnail. Reaching for a name for this lovely residue, I come up with "chitlins" — a colloquial term from the American South. If marinade, cooking time and planets have aligned correctly, the chitlin scrapings are to die for, and my thumbnail is the perfect utensil.

This sockeye whose flesh I so enjoy is a doorway to understanding a vast swath of marine and terrestrial ecology, from the cold depths of the North Pacific Ocean to the tidal estuaries and rainforests of the BC coast, and all the way to the dry interior river basins of the Columbia and the Fraser. Then, of course, there is the Sockeye That Stayed Home: the kokanee, which inhabits our Interior lakes with connections to the ocean. I had the privilege of getting up close and personal with the kokanee of Kootenay Lake in a previous book.

An icon of interconnectedness, the sockeye and its anadromous cousins — the chinook, the coho, the chum and the pink — touch the lives of literally hundreds of other species, from microscopic ocean copepods to cedar trees to grizzly bears. If nature handed out an award for ecological interconnectedness, the unassuming sockeye would win hands-down. The fish would also take another award — for greatest geographical range — since the sockeye reaches from the far end of the Aleutians to the distant headwaters of the Fraser and the Columbia. Although the fish's name gets full marks for Anglo-Saxon brevity and alliteration, it is totally inappropriate: *sockeye* is a settler corruption of the Coast Salish word *sukkai*, meaning "the fish of fishes."

The sockeye is a traditional vessel of human culture, but also a sleek and mobile fertilizer container. After two or three years in natal freshwater lakes and rivers, these remarkable fish head downstream to coastal estuaries and then out to sea, tracking along the coast of British Columbia and Alaska, and on to the Aleutian Islands. There, they feed on a veritable bestiary of tiny organisms that drift with the ocean currents. These plankton (from the Greek *plankter*, "to wander") offer up their bodies and nutrients to the sockeye. Once mature, the fish move on to the open ocean south of the Aleutians, eventually returning to their home river to spawn and die. Their carcasses contain a rich bounty of nitrogen, phosphorous, potassium, calcium, sulphur, carbon and other elements, all largely donated by Aleutian plankton. A recently hatched salmon fry contains about three milligrams of nitrogen. That same fish, returning from its ocean odyssey to spawn and die in its birthplace, contains three hundred grams of nitrogen.

Some of this organic bounty is passed on to the next generation of sockeye juveniles, but the rest — the mortal remains of dead and dying spawners — is foraged by a vast menagerie of algae, fungi, bacteria, protozoa, aquatic and terrestrial insects, herbaceous plants, trees, birds and mammals. The major players in this interspecies nutrient transfer are ravens, eagles, wolves, bears and blowflies. They feed on dead salmon along rivers and streambanks, then move the nutrients far afield via excreta and their own eventual death. Bears not only transport digested fish nutrients, they move live fish as well. Once Ms. Bear snags a sockeye spawner from the creek, she prefers to eat alone, without the distraction of uninvited dinner guests. To do this, she typically takes the captured fish away from the creekbank to the peace and quiet of the adjacent forest.

The headwater regions of British Columbia's streams and rivers are generally nutrient-poor, arising from granitic mountains or muskeg. Researchers have compared similar coastal streams — those which accommodate salmon spawning against those which do not — and the vegetation surrounding the spawning stream is demonstrably bigger and more diverse than that of a comparable but fishless stream. The source of this remarkable richness can be traced from the vegetation, back to the salmon, and all the way back to the Aleutian plankton. This is done using an ingenious scientific technique known as isotope discrimination. A naturally occurring variant of normal N14 nitrogen, known as N15, is preferentially absorbed by marine plankton. Because plankton are a major component of sockeye diet, the fish in turn have higher levels of N15. By comparing the ratios of N15 to N14 in terrestrial plant and animal species, researchers can determine whether salmon-derived nitrogen contributed to their growth. Fisheries scientists had long suspected this transfer of marine-derived nutrients (MDN) via salmon, but the advent of nitrogen isotope analysis provided an objective, quantitative basis for their research. The finding of higher N15 concentrations in the tissues of bears and ravens that feed directly on salmon was not surprising, but also finding it in river-edge cedar, western hemlock, huckleberry and salmonberry was truly a revelation. It almost makes one nostalgic for those bygone, interconnected days of Gaia.

As if MDN was not sexy enough on its own, imagine my delight when I discovered that tree rings are also involved. Tree growth, as measured by tree-ring widths, is faster along Alaskan rivers that host salmon spawners, and slower along rivers that do not. Okay, you say, but doesn't that just confirm what we already know from the nitrogen isotope work? Yes, but — and this is a very big *but* — coastal tree rings can take us back in salmon time to the 1800s, 1700s, even the 1500s if we are lucky.

Reliable records of salmon escapement (an unfortunate technical term referring to the number of spawners entering a river or stream) only go back a few decades. On top of that, escapement is subject to natural cycles. Southern sockeye runs are higher in odd-numbered years, in every fourth year, and during the negative phase of the thirty-year Pacific Decadal Oscillation, a climate cycle similar to El Niño. Tree rings, plus the nitrogen isotope work, allow us to backcast salmon trends, watershed by watershed, separating the natural impacts from human ones, leading to a better understanding of the uncertain future of this amazing fish, the one that I so casually consume.

Imagine, for a moment, the life of a pre-cannery, pre-dam, pre-logging, pre-pollution, pre-climate-change sockeye run in the Columbia River system. (While doing so, please tolerate the parenthetical salmon-nerd terminology that follows.) After its leisurely two-thousand-kilometre upstream swim, a gravid female (a spawner) arrives at the headwaters near Invermere in early fall. There, she searches out a gravel bed in shallow water. The particular water depth, speed and temperature are to her liking, as is the diameter of the gravels below. Using her tailfin, she scoops out a shallow basin in the gravel (a redd) and deposits her eggs (the roe). A male, hovering nearby and not helping with any of the housework, quickly moves over the redd to deposit his sperm (the milt). The female returns to cover the eggs with gravel. Shortly thereafter, both male and female spawners die and become sources of MDN. Next spring, a tiny infant sockeye (an alevin) hatches and hovers quietly within the gravel bed. Its nourishment comes from the egg yolk sac, which is still attached to its body. Once the yolk nutrients are exhausted, it emerges from the gravel as a tiny but fully formed fish (a fry). The main river channel is no safe place for a fry, but fortunately spring snowmelt in the Rockies swells the Columbia, so there are temporary shallow backwaters and off-channel floodplains — safe refuge and feeding habitat for this young fry. Here in the backwaters, the fry feeds on freshwater plankton and small insects until it is ready to venture back into the main channel, and to commence its monumental trek downstream to the ocean (as a smolt). Then it makes the remarkable transition from fresh water to salt water (a sea run salmon), cruising and feeding in the North

Pacific. After a given number of years — typically, five to seven years after birth — it returns to the same stretch of the mother Columbia as a spawner.

Notice in this brief life-cycle description that no definitive time periods are given. Salmon follow a bewildering variety of life-cycle event timing, depending on species, runs, river and year.

As I studied the pioneering scientific papers that first described the MDN phenomenon, I found their tone predictably matter-of-fact and coldly unemotional, but so be it. I suppose the more groundbreaking and controversial the research, the more subdued and objective the language becomes. But these same scientists did come up with some intriguing new catchphrases, like "cross-boundary nutrient subsidies," "isotopic evidence," "trophic cascades," and "cultural oligotrophication."

This last phrase definitely caught my attention, We contemporary humans, through our profligate culture of dams, climate change, overfishing, deforestation, channellization, oil spills, microplastics and spawning bed siltation, are reducing salmon runs and thus impoverishing (*oligo* = "few") headwater terrestrial ecosystems.

This oligotrophication notion seemed pretty abstract to me until I discovered California research that found N15 in wine grapes. My Chardonnay is local, not a Californian, but alarm bells went off. Could our own Okanagan vineyards be extracting the last fossil N15 from the once abundant — and now impoverished — salmon runs in the Okanagan River system? What if this bizarre and wonderful connection from sockeye to eagle to ponderosa pine to *Vitis vinifera* is irreparably broken? If there is a god and she is listening, please make us fix this.

Our Okanagan River is part of the massive Columbia River watershed, a fact that is frequently ignored, since the Okanagan joins the Columbia on the American side of the border. As a watershed, it has been massively impacted. There are some two hundred and fifty dams on the Columbia main stem and its tributaries. As one writer commented, "The Columbia does not flow, it is operated." Each dam poses a partial or total obstacle to salmon spawners heading upstream, plus a number of hazards for smolts heading downstream. Contemplate the yearly loss of MDNs to that entire river system, then conservatively multiply that by forty years of existing dam life, and you have the math for cultural oligotrophication on a continental scale, not to mention the salmon overharvesting.

Fortunately, our Okanagan River system branches off from the Columbia before it reaches the two salmon-killer dams, Chief Joseph and Grand Coulee, so a few spawning sockeye do actually make it past the nine other dams between the mouth of the Columbia and the Okanagan confluence. These nine are Bonneville, Dalles, John Day, McNary, Priest Rapids, Rocky Reach, Rock Island, Wanapum and Wells. But even after successfully reaching the Okanagan River, the sockeye are confronted with other obstacles: the shallow and rapidly warming Osoyoos Lake; the Zosel, McIntyre and Penticton dams; and the dead-straight, riprapped banks of the Okanagan system's river portions, which permanently gutted spawning habitat.

Once out of mountains and into a valley, rivers meander. It is in their nature. Meander shapes and sizes can actually be predicted using fluid dynamics, but I am more drawn to their poetry. I'm standing near the McAlpine Bridge, where Highway 97 crosses the Okanagan River north of the town of Oliver. By sheer act of will, I shut out the whine of cars and look north to a very short natural reach, one of very few left to this river. Dense vegetation crowds the banks. Amid the chaotic jumble of greenery, there is a rough ordering by height: the shorter species hug the riverbank, the taller are farther back. First comes rose, then willow, then aspen, and finally, towering cottonwoods. The riverbed itself is a celebration of sinuosity. Upstream, a point bar crowds the river over to the opposite bank. Below that, a comma-shaped island splits the water into a fast, riffling main channel and a slower, deeper side channel. Everything here is transitioning. Yesterday's gravel beach is tomorrow's grassy island. A riverbank is thick with rosebushes one day, and the next, it collapses to become bottom sediment. A bend becomes a cutoff oxbow. This is free-verse meander.

The Sky and the Patio

I trudge up the length of a gravel bar that is dry now but would have been submerged during spring runoff. The gravel itself has a bleached-white coating of dead algae. As I walk, I see the gravel diameters subtly change: smaller piece sizes at the downstream end of the bar, larger ones at the upstream end, all sorted by changing water velocities. Salmon spawners have definite preferences for certain intermediate sizes of gravel, and certain water depths and velocities. Meanders alone provide that choice.

Farther along, the meander's slow side channel draws my eye. The bleached skeleton of a big cottonwood veteran lies across its lower end, half submerged. The tree's massive rootwad has collected sticks and branches from previous freshets. Just downstream of the rootwad is a deep, quiet pool, a place of momentary rest for sojourning spawners.

A carefully timed sprint across busy 97 takes me to the south side of the bridge, where a totally different story unfolds. Here, the channellized river is narrow, straight and fast — no gravel bars, no meanders. Non-native trees grow along the confined banks, and the telltale shoulders of riprap boulders show through. This channellized stretch is identical to the other ninety percent of the Okanagan system's precious river portions.

The Okanagan is a curious system, more lake than river. From its modest headwaters around Armstrong, it trends southward through the accordion-folded terrain of the eponymous valley, becoming lake, then river, then lake, then river, and finally morphing to its last lake at Osoyoos. The Okanagan (both the valley and the river) becomes the Okanogan, as it crosses the US border. (The difference in spelling of the original Syilx name is not surprising; one historian amassed some fifty different settler spellings of the word.) The Similkameen River joins the Okanogan just south of the border, and a hundred kilometres farther southward the Okanogan finally merges with the Columbia.

Back in my car, I continue driving south on the 97. Here too, the river has been completely stripped of its creativity, becoming an orderly, carefully engineered ditch. The riprapped banks, a

A Paean to the Sockeye

response to flooding in the 1940s, are slide-ruled to perfection, running either dead straight or in neatly bevelled curves. No gravels, no bars, no sheltering rootwads, nothing graces the channel except the occasional concrete "drop structure." (Somehow, this is different than a dam.)

Stopping just north of the town of Oliver, I see a ray of hope for this river, one of the most endangered in Canada. Here, a small group of visionary hydrologists and fish biologists abandoned the traditional river dogma of Dike, Dam, Denude and Develop, to create a new school of engineering. Their teacher was the river itself. They learned the complex and shifting geometry of meanders. They found the shallow graves of old pre-channellization point bars and oxbows. They studied the needs of spawners. With patience and persistence, they assembled funding, adjacent land and multiple permissions. They filled out reams of paper and explained their project a thousand times. Then they moved the channel's riprap dikes back, from twenty metres apart to one hundred. And they re-meandered.

The flood control function is still in place, but here this three-kilometre stretch of river has been given back a semblance of its original life. It now has room to write its poetry, to move its gravels and silts, to place its rootwads and riffles and rapids in those particular messy arrangements to which ten millennia of spawning salmon have grown accustomed.

The city of Penticton sits on a pleasant isthmus between Okanagan and Skaha lakes. The twelve-kilometre stretch of the Okanagan River that runs between the two lakes — and right through the middle of town — was straightened and channellized in the 1950s. The Channel, as it is now called, is summer habitat for a very abundant species known as the tuber. The typical life cycle of a tuber pack starts at the dollar store near the upstream end of the Channel, where a $29.95 multi-person inflatable plastic raft is purchased. Next stop is the adjacent liquor store for a two-four, and then over to the launch site at the Channel's edge. Several hours and beers later, the tubers (*Homo inflatabilis var. molsonii*) arrive at the disembarkation point, where the Channel empties into Skaha Lake. Then the pack pays a few bucks for a ride in an ancient repurposed school bus to return to their start point. This remarkable aspect of human ecology can be seen anytime between June and September, with an emphasis on weekends.

River channellization not only destroys meanders, it eliminates springtime floodplains. Temporary high-water floodplains and backwaters are safe havens and rich feeding grounds for young salmon fry. As the high water slowly recedes, the bulked-up and emboldened fry are then ready to move back into the main channel. These adjacent floodplains, as crucial to salmon as the gravel spawning beds, were another victim of channellization.

An innovative floodplain re-creation project between the Penticton Indian Band and the Okanagan Nation Alliance is under way near the En'owkin Centre, on the Penticton Indian Reserve. The west side of the channel has been breached, and a shallow, carefully configured two-hectare catch basin is being created to hold both spring high water and sockeye fry.

In local Syilx tradition, Coyote led Sockeye, Chinook, Coho and Steelhead up from the Pacific Ocean to the Okanagan. Then came the dam spasm — an era of concrete, riprap and fish hatcheries — and the salmon all but disappeared. Now it is the men and women of the Okanagan River Restoration Initiative, and the Okanagan Nation Alliance, that are bringing the fish back. They are patient. They do it one spawning bed, one meander, one floodplain, one river poem at a time.

My local Summerland grocery store has a butcher shop, so they keep their salmon fillets on a bed of ice instead of in the ubiquitous plastic or Styrofoam trays. I get to pick the best-looking fillets from the row of twenty or so, and when I get home I take pleasure in extracting the fillet from the wax paper the butcher wrapped it in. Not only is this a pleasant reminder of childhood trips to the butcher shop with my mom, but it also lets me thumb my nose at the ubiquitous Canadian food-plastics industry.

A Paean to the Sockeye

I once ordered fillets from another supermarket, but wasn't watching when the butcher packaged it. He handed it to me on a black Styrofoam tray wrapped in plastic film. I took sadistic pleasure in saying to him, "Have you ever heard of butcher paper?"

The future of sockeye, like the future of many British Columbia creatures and habitats, is in doubt. Should I, as an individual consumer, support an ethical salmon fishery, or should I register my concern by no longer buying my beloved salmon fillets? I put this question to a well-known salmon expert. His pained and conflicted answer was: "I don't know."

This evening I have taken the extra time to cook some Saskatchewan wild rice (Cree: *manôminak*) to accompany the pan-seared sockeye. They are elegant on the plate and pair perfectly on the palate. As I scrape the last of the chitlins and finish the Chardonnay, I imagine one sockeye's pre-dam journey from the Aleutians down to the mouth of the Columbia, then up through the semi-desert of the Columbia Basin, finally detouring north up the Okanagan River, to spawn and die not far from where I sit. Another envisioned sockeye stays in the Columbia and travels all the way to its headwater lake at Invermere. Yet another swims up the Fraser River to Prince George, then west on the Nechako, and north again on the Stuart to spawn and die in Stuart Lake. A fish like this deserves more than recipes and rituals. It deserves rescue.

Toasting the sockeye that sacrificed its flesh for me, I raise my nearly empty glass. It is the less breakable, stemless type, a truncated egg shape lightly coated with fish oil fingerprints. A good lens through which to look at the mute and troubled evening sky.

10
GIVING NATURE A VOICE

HIKING THESE OKANAGAN hills, I often fall prey to landscape trickery. After a steep uphill grind, my chosen hill finally starts to level out. Elated, I think the weight-loss clinic is nearly over and the summit, or at least a scenic ridge, is near. Certainly, there will be a restful rock to sit upon while I contemplate transcendental views. But no: this hill has deceived me, offering just a small, forested plateau with another steep rise above it, followed by another plateau and steep rise. This trickery leads me to abandon the hike in disgust, or continue it out of sheer orneriness, plus the promise of the minor visual rewards of each new plateau. This choice depends on my state of mind, the ambient temperature, and whether there is lunch in the backpack.

Geologist Stuart Holland, in his 1964 volume *Landforms of British Columbia*, identifies the Okanagan Highland as extending from the town of Vernon south into Washington State. He describes it as a landform of "rounded mountains and ridges and gentle open slopes on an upland surface." Only from a distance could our landforms be described as rounded and gentle. Up close is another story entirely.

Climbing straight up a hill is a stupid human habit, shared only with rabbits. Every other land mammal travels along the contour, making zigzag trails that ascend at a comfortable ten to fifteen degrees above or below the horizontal. These are the trails I mostly follow, but my physiotherapist says my calf muscles are tight and I need to stretch them by leaning forward, one leg at a time, with

The Sky and the Patio

my heel planted. So I do this by occasionally departing from the game trail and going straight uphill, until I hit the next one.

In remote areas, one very occasionally sees a steep, grassy hillside with a series of closely spaced parallel trails running across the slope. These are made by a rarely observed nocturnal mammal known as the Sidehill Gouger (*Membriinequales declivitous*), whose legs on the left side of its body are shorter than on the right side.

The actual four-footers who make these Okanagan trails have great landscape wisdom. They arrange them to pass through moist glens, open vantage points and scree slopes. No matter the compass direction I want to pursue, or whether I wish to go upslope or down, a few minutes' search always yields a suitable game trail. Often it is just a faint winding strip of bare ground a few centimetres wide, just wide enough for the delicate hooves of muleys and whitetails. My hooves are size 14, so I struggle a bit, but no matter. It is refreshing to know there are still a few objects in this world not scaled for the human.

I recently discovered the local landscape trickery also works in reverse, when I explored the botany of Marron Valley, a narrow side valley paralleling the main Okanagan. I was intrigued by this little valley because its eponymous watercourse is British Columbia's smallest official river — you can jump across it — and because of its unusual name. This word reaches back to the French *marron* ("wild, feral") and to the Spanish *cimarron* (same meaning), with a derivation *maroon* (an escaped slave). Pioneering settler botanist David Douglas passed through this valley in 1833, naming its watercourse the River of Wild Horses. In 1871, the name was officially changed to Marron River, neatly tying together borrowed words, ambiguity of meaning, and wild horses of Spanish origin.

I was contemplating this etymology as I casually descended the Marron Valley's first gentle upper slope. I should have suspected landscape trickery as I hit a downward inflection, but a dense stand of ponderosas obscured what lay below me. The valley's downward curve soon went from gradual to geometric. Two hours later, after several backtracks, hanging on to branches and mostly sliding down loose and stony game trails winding in between vertical rockbluffs, I reached the bottom of the valley and its littlest river. Botanizing was impossible, as all the riparian vegetation had been destroyed by wild horses, probably descendants of the ones Douglas saw two centuries ago.

In addition to ups and downs, hiking engages a series of faculties and states of mind in a kind of progression. My hikes start out with a modest sense of liberation from computers and the mundane workday. Almost immediately, my autonomous taxonomy motor fires up, compulsively identifying plants and struggling to recall their scientific names. Then, due to a long scientific association with native grasses, I start estimating the percentage cover of the three or four dominant species. Meanwhile, another mental side channel is attentive to changes in aspect and soil type, another is alert for fossils and arrowheads, while yet another slice of consciousness focuses on potential rattlesnake or bear encounters. Then I start to speculate on geological time — how long has this landscape been an alternation of grassland, parkland forest, closed forest, riparian meadow and bald knob, draped over a volcanic and glaciated earth?

There is a drive, almost an instinct, that pushes us from facts toward abstractions. Can we push that drive even further, from scientific abstraction to romantic poetry? Or to the deification of the nature that we simultaneously study and destroy?

As the hike progresses, the faint but liberating odour of ponderosa pine sap starts me thinking about process: the hidden software that nature runs on. Succession. Disturbance. Flowering sequence. Interspecies nutrient transfers. Seed dispersal, symbiosis and so on. But these too turn out to be more scientific urgencies, just at a more abstracted level. Eventually, I get to thinking about pattern, and evidence of design. A delicately symmetric feather, separated from its owner. The Fibonacci spiral of a native sunflower. The endlessly variable landscape patterns of balsamroot and bunchgrass, sagebrush and saskatoon, moss and lichen, ponderosa pine and Douglas-fir, rock outcrop and gully. The timeless feel of this hillside, clothed in Wyoming big sagebrush and bluebunch wheatgrass. It speaks

The Sky and the Patio

of no human presence, and yet here I am. And I know this hillside has experienced Indigenous cultural burning events.

Then things get marginally weird when I ask myself what I'm doing here. Am I part of nature, or separate from it? Do I have a choice in this matter? Is it fair to say that humans have ethics, which we frequently ignore, but nature has no ethics? Has nature achieved some infinitely complex ecological balance over the millennia, that serves in lieu of ethics? The sandhill cranes might know the answer. They have the perspective of time, and distance.

So now I have followed the game trails to this isolated location, sat myself comfortably on a chosen rock, and allowed the daily dross to fall away. Yet I sense my thoughts turning inward, rather than outward. As John Muir said, a going out into nature is actually a going in. Why is that? Am I seeing this landscape through some very specific, western-settler lens? Can I try out other lenses, like when I go to the optometrist? Is my view of nature somehow a product of literature? This is quite likely, given my bookishness. As the brilliant historian Simon Schama says, "Landscapes are culture before they are nature." So a devoted amateur's brief and personal tracing of the evolution of western views of nature, through the lens of literature, is a pleasant exercise.

The ancient Greeks gave us the concept of pastoralism. This was a comforting retreat into rural agriculture as an antidote to the political intrigues, corruption and bad sanitation of metropolitan Athens. Theocritus, Ovid, Virgil and others all praised the rural, bucolic lifestyle. But it is important to note that pastoralism was not really about farming, it was about herding. With animals, in nature. In pastoralism, the shepherd — idle, sensual, half-wild — was the hero. That pastoral thread is permanently woven into our western relationship with nature, although it has waxed and waned over the centuries.

The Bible gave us all manner of mixed messages about nature, but the dominant one decreed that man (very specifically, the male of the species) has dominion over nature. The Dark Ages and the medieval era produced the concept of nature as evil; nature as a dark and scary place, to be dreaded and avoided. This thread persists too, mostly in children's books and in horror movies.

Then, in the late 1700s — the Age of Enlightenment — the Frenchman Jean-Jacques Rousseau came to the fore. Rousseau claimed that humans are inherently good, but are corrupted by human institutions. Therefore, the way for the individual to remain virtuous is to spend solitary time in nature. His model was the Wolf-boy of Aveyron, an orphan child found living on his own in the woods. Of course, Rousseau was dismissed as a hopeless romantic, but this thread, of finding morality and comfort in nature, stays with us as well.

Along the way, there have been periodic assertions of nature as female, or nature as sacred *and* female. As one commentator put it, if men nursed babies, there would be no wars. Unfortunately, these ideas have never gotten much traction in western thought. The rape continues.

Nature is in fact infinite, unpredictable, generous, brutal and unknowable in its entirety. That puts it squarely in the realm of the spiritual, a realm some skeptics refer to as the "woo woo shit." We do seem to have trouble embracing any kind of spirituality that stands outside of organized theistic religion.

Are humans part of nature? That is an interesting philosophical question. One answer is that at one time we were, but then we invented cellphones. We humans need a set of morals and ethics to operate, whereas nature does not. We often see nature as a source of morals, so it is difficult to accept it as amoral. But in fact nature is simply an enormous set of organisms and relationships playing out over time in terrestrial and aquatic habitats. The time factor — the eons — confers stability, resilience and reciprocality to nature's relationships.

The 1780s saw the publication of *The Natural History of Selborne*, by the Englishman Gilbert White, pioneer birdwatcher and companion to Timothy the tortoise. This book probably stands as the first example of what we would now call nature writing. Here is how White introduces himself:

> The Author takes the liberty of laying before the public his idea of parochial history, which, he thinks, ought to consist of natural productions and occurrences. He is also of opinion that stationary men should pay some attention to the districts on which they reside.

What a wonderfully laconic prescription for actually living in one's home place, which for White was a village in the farming country southwest of London. I am fortunate to own an undated early edition of *Natural History*, which as far as I can tell was printed in 1879. It is a small book, likely designed to fit in the side pocket of a man's tweed jacket. The binding is yellowed and the pages are thin and fragile, like tissue paper. The book is 470 pages long, but surprisingly it is just over an inch thick, due to the thinness of the paper. Both the book and its contents speak of a forgotten era.

Then came George Perkins Marsh (1801–1882), a Vermonter who could perhaps be called the first ecologist:

> All Nature is linked together by invisible bonds and every organic creature....is necessary to the well-being of some other among the myriad forms of life.

Marsh also pioneered the notion that human activities can affect climate.

Henry David Thoreau (1817–1862) and his book *Walden* became the standard against which all other nature writing has been measured. Thoreau introduced and legitimized personal and spiritual retreats into nature. He was also the master of the quotable quote:

> It's not what you look at that matters, it's what you see.

> Many men go fishing all of their lives without knowing that it is not fish they are after.
>
> Disobedience is the true foundation of liberty.

Walt Whitman (1819–1892), a contemporary of Thoreau, was a Transcendentalist. Here's a snippet from one of his poems:

> When the full-grown poet came,
> Out spake pleased Nature (the round impassive globe, with all its shows of day and night,) saying, *He is mine*;
> But out spake too the Soul of man, proud, jealous and unreconciled, *Nay, he is mine alone*;
> —Then the full-grown poet stood between the two, and took each by the hand;
> And to-day and ever so stands, as blender, uniter, tightly holding hands,
> Which he will never release until he reconciles the two,
> And wholly and joyously blends them.

Whitman was celebratory, and pansexual. A lover of men and a worshipper of women. An everyman, and yet a solitary poet. A patriot and an internationalist. A critical thinker and a Dionysian hedonist. A pacifist and an unabashed feminist. A nature lover and an urbanite.

Reading Whitman is like reading the Bible: for every conceivable human situation, he has some resonant and thoughtful phrase. Whenever I am in need of reassurance about what it means to be a man, I go back to Whitman.

I like to remind myself that both Thoreau and Whitman were city-dwellers, or rather town-dwellers. They lived in a place and time when urban concentrations had small footprints, and relatively unspoiled nature was within walking distance of their town's centre. So Whitman, for instance, could spend an idle day wandering in the woods, write a bit, and then return to the town's pub in the evening to drink and carouse with his friends. This is the origin of my First Axiom of Urban Planning: the downtown pub must be within walking distance of the woods.

John Muir (1838–1914) was a passionate advocate for wilderness, and wrote dozens of essays and descriptions of nature, many of them centred around the Sierra Mountains of California. He is the spiritual godfather of the US national park system.

These three, Thoreau, Whitman and Muir, injected personal spirituality into their relationship with nature, and this has had a lasting influence. One theory has it that these men replaced the traditional European places of worship — the cathedrals — with New World old-growth forests. Ironically, earlier generations of Europeans who designed the uplifting, vertically oriented architecture of those same cathedrals drew their inspiration from remnant European old-growth forests.

In spite of their tremendous talents, these three nature writers mistakenly saw wilderness as pristine and devoid of human influence. This fit well with the self-serving settler view of North America as an essentially empty, untouched continent, patiently awaiting the fruits of European civilization. Some of those rotten fruits are with us today.

It is true that these writers who found spiritual solace in nature favoured those outdoor locations that were safe and congenial to the visiting human. As the irascible essayist Aldous Huxley pointed out, referring to another romantic poet, William Wordsworth:

> The Wordsworthian who exports this pantheistic
> worship of Nature to the tropics is liable to have his
> religious convictions somewhat rudely disturbed.

Aldo Leopold (1887–1948) wove his profession of wildlife biology into his writing about rural Wisconsin, in *A Sand County Almanac*. Rachel Carson (1907–1964), in *Silent Spring* and *The Sea Around Us*, wrote the first cry for help. She was a literal voice in the wilderness. Carson's books probably represent the earliest example of what we now call environmental writing.

Loren Eiseley (1907–1977) blended science and often painfully personal introspection quite beautifully. His short piece "The Star Thrower," set on a lonely Mexican beach, is a classic of the essay form. Leopold, Carson and particularly Eiseley were able combine science and lyrical description within the same narrative.

This is a very American list: we Canadians have traditionally lived very close to nature, and perhaps because of that, we have not been so inspired to write about it. But there are three notable exceptions. The Canadian-American Wallace Stegner (1909–1993) wrote beautifully in *Wolf Willow* about coming back to the little Prairie town of Eastend, Saskatchewan, where he grew up:

> It is a country to breed mystical people, egocentric people, perhaps poetic people. But not humble ones...Puny you may feel there, and vulnerable, but not unnoticed. This is a land to mark the sparrow's fall.

Farley Mowat's (1921–2014) book *Never Cry Wolf* is iconic, perhaps our most prized piece of Canadian nature writing. Another Canadian, Stan Rowe (1918–2004), wrote an influential book, *Home Place: Essays on Ecology*. Stan, in his typically modest way, pointed out a flaw in our thinking about nature, in an essay called "Biological Fallacy: Life Equals Organisms." Life, he said, cannot be separated from the inanimate habitat that surrounds it.

Two American writers, Annie Dillard and Barry Lopez (1945–2020), were the Joan Baez and Bob Dylan of nature writing. These two represent the modern apogee of traditional nature writing, with the publication of Dillard's *Pilgrim at Tinker Creek* in 1974 and a series of fine books by Lopez in the late '70s and early '80s.

Then came the concept of deep ecology, put forward by Arne Naess (1912–2009). Remember deep ecology, which was supposed to put humans on an equal footing with other organisms? That, along with the Age of Gaia, lasted about as long as a fart in a windstorm.

The ecological restoration movement was next, attempting to bring humans closer to nature by enlisting us to repair ecosystems we have damaged. That movement is still around, and I have great and nostalgic admiration for it, and for the writings of its main proponent, William Jordan. But ecological restoration is now a fringe movement at best.

Educator Richard Louv defined the nature deficit disorder, and the nefarious impact of new digital technologies that impose

The Sky and the Patio

a barrier between us and nature. But I want to put this technology barrier into a historical context. Leo Marx (1919–2022), in his book aptly entitled *The Machine in the Garden*, relates a story about Nathaniel Hawthorne, a New England poet from the 1840s. Hawthorne is spending a romantic day out in nature, enjoying the leaves and the trees and the sun and the birds, when his nature reverie is rudely shattered by the harsh shriek of a train whistle, produced by the brand new technology of the steam locomotive. So is an iPad, and the digital world it contains, a bigger intrusion than a locomotive? I guess my point is that our endless progression of new technologies has been inserting itself between us and nature for quite some time.

The writer Bill Plotkin suggests that true adulthood is achieved by developing a relationship with nature. This makes our contemporary tech-driven society by definition adolescent.

The grand tradition of romantic nature writing experienced a tectonic shift in the 1980s and 1990s, with the belated and gut-wrenching awareness of our human impacts on the planet. This shift was summed up very succinctly by the Canadian writer Moira Farr, in a 1993 essay entitled "The Death of Nature Writing":

> Only a very naïve or dishonest writer would head off today into what he or she took to be the unspoiled wilderness, and engage with it in the manner of a Dillard or a Thoreau. It would be self-indulgent, to say the least, to write of one's communion with a mighty river, while failing to mention the last remaining fish in it bulge with cancerous tumours. A contemporary writer would probably hesitate to find in leaves, vegetable mould or maple keys uplifting metaphors for the transcendent self; at the edge of the imagination sways a chorus of furies crying Acid Rain! Global Warming! Deforestation! Desertification! Dead Dolphins in Drift Nets! Species Extinction! Nuclear Meltdown! Dioxins in your breast milk!

The contemporary American writer Robin Wall Kimmerer has come at nature writing from a committed Indigenous perspective in *Braiding Sweetgrass*. And one of BC's very own, Suzanne Simard, has put a fascinating feminist frame around the male bastion of forestry in *Finding the Mother Tree*.

I find it hard to let go of the rhapsodic and emotional attachments to nature that Thoreau, Whitman and the rest have conjured up. Natural landscapes have provided me with both refuge and inspiration over the course of my lifetime. I can project all my intimate personal feelings and bonds into these mountains and meadows and grasslands, knowing all the while they don't give a damn about me. Their total lack of reciprocal empathy is comforting, in a certain way.

In this brief overview, I have bypassed painting as a major influence on our nature relation, but will acknowledge a single artist, Albert Bierstadt (1830–1902). A contemporary of Muir and a mere generation after Whitman and Thoreau, he literally turned their words into transcendental images. His paintings of Yosemite are profoundly romantic, but magnificent in their own right. One cannot mention Bierstadt without also referring to Kent Monkman, a contemporary Indigenous Canadian painter who has turned the Bierstadt Yosemite image delightfully on its ear.

Photographers have also had a modern impact on our nature views: foremost among those, of course, is Ansel Adams (1902–1984). More recently, the Canadian photographer Edward Burtynsky is the visual poet of the industrial mayhem we visit upon the earth.

Back in the 1990s, the British Columbia government sponsored a series of regional land use planning exercises. I participated in one called the Kootenay-Boundary Land Use Plan. The plan was developed through dozens of stakeholder meetings around the region, where various land use metrics were discussed and adopted. We worked through measures like stems per hectare, kilometres of roads per hectare, hunter days per hectare, cows per hectare and so on, which we could then use to better manage the landscapes of the Kootenays and the Boundary country. I came up with a proposed new metric, called epiphanies per hectare. It was unanimously voted down.

I have great respect for First Nations worldviews about nature, but those worldviews are proprietary, and I can't be a surrogate. There are two reasons for this. First, I am an obvious Irish-Norwegian mixed breed, and second, I don't like cultural appropriation. So my job is twofold. First is to make space, whenever I can, for Indigenous folks to tell their own stories. Second is to search out any roots of my own Anglo culture that have given standing to nature. However, those nature beliefs reside so far back in historical time that to weave them into contemporary culture is a long shot; Druid or Viking worldviews are marginally useful today. So if I can't find any compelling nature beliefs from within my own cultural ancestry, then I damn well have to create a set of new ones.

Here lies the dilemma of the landed Canadian settler. Indigenous and European cultures, for example, evolved within their own regional landscapes. A Syilx or a Dane or a Latvian can walk through native woods and meadows knowing her ancient ancestors and their culture were shaped by the very leaves she touches with contemporary hands. In sharp contrast, we Canadian settlers have at most a century and a half of that crucial landscape experience, and for many who landed in urban settings, little or none at all. I have been working on a personal worldview called Honky Agnostic Land-Based Mysticism. Recently, I decided that title doesn't quite capture the essence. So now I'm crafting a variant called Honky Agnostic Land-Based Science-Infused Mysticism (HALBSIM). It is definitely a work in progress.

It is late and my time on the sitting rock is over. I start heading back in my usual fashion, taking a totally different route and seeing how close I can come to where I parked the car. Dead reckoning, I call it — one of my few talents. This homeward walk prompts an appropriate literary closing, in the form of Edna St. Vincent Millay's poem "Afternoon on a Hill":

> I will be the gladdest thing
> Under the sun!

I will touch a hundred flowers
   And not pick one.

I will look at cliffs and clouds
   With quiet eyes.
Watch the wind bow down the grass
   And the grass rise.

And when lights begin to show
   Up from the town,
I will mark which must be mine
   And then start down!

11
SHAMBALA, FEMINIZATION AND GREAT GREEN FURBALLS

IN OCTOBER OF 2018, Canada legalized marijuana, finally acknowledging a long-established reality. The year 2018 was notable in another regard: that was when the Intergovernmental Panel on Climate Change told us we had twelve years to go before we reached an irreversible climate change tipping point. I wonder if there is a connection.

I hadn't grown dope for many years, but after the federal announcement I felt it was not only my right but my duty as a red-blooded Canadian baby boomer to grow no more than four legal plants — for medically related home consumption only.

Early the next spring, I bought five seeds for an absolutely outrageous price, and started them indoors. The new law stipulated that the plants could not be "in public view," so when it came time to transplant, I tucked the three surviving seedlings into a planter in the far backyard, behind a grapevine row, together with several tomato plants for cover.

I had forgotten how aggressive *Cannabis sativa* plants can be. They soon overwhelmed the poor tomato plants, completely dominated the planter, and threatened to be in public view of the street, in spite of a house, a fence and a vineyard in between. I remembered a vintage photo of a friend of mine from the old days. He was standing in his rural marijuana patch outside of Edmonton, and the tops of the plants were about a metre above his head. His plants were all lanky and single-stalked, probably closely related to the ancestral rope variety, whereas mine, in spring 2019, were

The Sky and the Patio

enormously fat, like great green exploding furballs, with flowering side stems arising from every leaf axil.

There is a personal irony here: indulging in the tremendously potent "wheelchair dope" of today, I have decided I kind of miss the low-grade stems and leaves we smoked in the '60s.

Canada has traditionally had a more relaxed and adult approach to cannabis, communists, draft resisters and alcohol than our neighbour to the south. The US Prohibition era, which lasted thirteen long years, from 1920 to 1933, was a huge financial boon to Canadian entrepreneurs living close to the US border. The author Wallace Stegner, who grew up during that era, wrote about big Fords with heavy-duty suspensions and blinkered headlights moving nighttime cases of Canadian whisky south across the remote Saskatchewan-Montana border. My wife's grandfather was a purser on the Black Ball Ferry that ran between Victoria and Seattle during Prohibition, and he used his two young daughters as mules. Ostensibly returning from pleasure trips to Victoria with their dad, and cold from the ferry ride, they would arrive at the Seattle terminal bundled up in long coats. The sleeves of their coats were full of whisky bottles instead of arms. Family legend has it that the girls had to walk very slowly through customs to avoid making the telltale sound of clinking glass.

America's glorious late '60s era of pot, peace, love, Janis Joplin and tie-dye ran head-on into the criminal and ultimately tragic war in Vietnam. Young men — my baby boomer brethren — were caught in an absolutely Faustian triangle. Our fathers had served in World War II, one of history's more just wars, and patriotism ran strong through our households. Then came the Age of Aquarius and the endless possibilities of the '60s, immediately followed by the Vietnam War, with its daily draft notices and body counts. As a result, many of us moved to the quietly welcoming country of Canada. No one knows for sure how many came — maybe 30,000, maybe 70,000, or possibly 58,200, the number of our brother soldiers pointlessly killed in Vietnam. One of the many things we war resisters brought to Canada, to places like the Gulf Islands or the Slocan Valley, were cannabis seeds. Such are the origins of the justly famous BC Bud. These bearded hippies and their dreadlocked partners settled in and taught themselves the ancient arts of husbandry and crop selection. Year after year, they sampled and selected individual plants, slowly moving cannabis genetics away from its fibrous hemp origins toward dozens of individual varieties, all more floral and resinous than their industrial forebears.

One of the debts we owe to these bearded hippie dope growers is for their delightful contributions to, and reinterpretations of, the English language. *Spliff, doob, ganja, shake, reefer, toke, mary jane, fattie, joint, lid, bong, baggie, baked, kief, kush, bogart, roach, hermie.* This is just a sampling of street-level consumer words; the technical terms serious growers use are another linguistic universe unto itself.

Feminization (possibly together with feminism) gave BC Bud growers a profoundly important tool. Cannabis naturally produces female plants and male plants in about a 50/50 ratio, but the females contain all the good stuff — THC and cannabinoids. And furthermore, you don't want the males pollinating the females, since that makes the female plants lose their potency. Sad to say, the males are pretty much useless, but it is agonizingly late in the growing season before you can tell the sexes apart. Just imagine all the effort, not to mention water and fertilizer, that got wasted on males.

Plant feminization treatments have been known for a long time, but it was in the 1980s that BC Bud growers began to use them, to great advantage. Once a female plant is identified, it can be stressed to induce it to produce male pollen sacs, thus making the plant AC/DC and able to self-impregnate. That gravid plant is then allowed to mature and set "feminized" seed, ninety percent of which will then give rise to female plants. When the going gets tough, the women step up.

Cloning was another major milestone in the cannabis industry, where cuttings are taken from selected plants and grown out, thus preserving the exact genetics of the mother plant. But cloning is not for the backyard grower.

For some fifty years, let's say from 1968 to 2018, BC Bud strains were developed completely free of corporate involvement. No patents, no advertising, no boards of directors, no TSX, no GMO, no IPO, no enormous greenhouses and, for the most part, no herbicides. All that changed on October 18, 2018. If you want to learn about cannabis now, you go to the financial and business sections of our national newspapers.

One of the great mysteries of the pot industry here is the staggering number of retail stores. For example, our town of twelve thousand souls has *four* outlets. Each one has a blank, closed storefront. These, together with the equally omnipresent real estate offices, create urban dead zones.

Now that big business is involved, cannabis production is moving rapidly from small, seasonal, open-air plots to massive high-security greenhouses that use hydroponics as a growth medium, and operate year-round. Corporate cannabis is also quite willing to prey on rural communities that have lost traditional sources of employment and are desperate for jobs.

The product that comes out of those corporate facilities will be much like the supermarket tomato you buy in February: an elaborately constructed but flavourless replicate of the real thing. But the legions of British Columbians who grow their own tomatoes will recognize and value the difference, and interplant Sweet Skunk or Maui Wowie or BC Kush alongside their Romas and Early Girls. Fight back against corporate cannabis and plant four. If you can grow tomatoes, you can grow pot. But as you work out your plant spacing, be sure to visualize giant green furballs.

Much is written about the two strains, *sativa* and *indica*. Sativa generates the cerebral high, indica the corporeal. Although they are presented as two different species, they easily hybridize, and many of the current products on the market are, in fact, hybrids.

Nelson, BC, our home for many years, has always had a vibrant hippie and marijuana subculture. It is the funky hub for outlier communities in the Slocan Valley, the West Arm and Kootenay Lake. Some say Nelson actually exists in a kind of '60s time warp. The town's busy main thoroughfare is Baker Street, often referred to as Baked Street. One warm summer day, I was walking down Baker with my friend Larry, a long-bearded denizen of the Slocan Valley. Two tourists stopped us and asked directions to the Slocan. I deferred to Larry, who stroked his beard thoughtfully. After a long pause, he said, "The Slocan Valley is more a concept than it is a place," and then he continued walking.

Logging, for and against, is a perennial issue in Nelson, and one individual wrote to the local paper saying that logging would be more acceptable if we planted cannabis in the clear-cuts. Kind of a have-our-cake-and-eat-it-too option. As a licensed agronomist, I took issue and wrote a reasoned response to the letter, saying that for all its benefits, cannabis is a soil miner, would encourage soil erosion and is definitely not a suitable crop for a forest clear-cut. My letter came out just before Shambala, Nelson's famous annual outdoor music/drug fest. One of my sons, a late teenager at the time, came back and reported that I had been hung in effigy at Shambala. I'm still not sure if I should be honoured or offended by that.

You can buy a bottle of Okanagan wine for ten bucks or a hundred bucks; different wineries, varieties, years and prices make for a delightfully large range of possible choices. Over time, the cannabis sector will likely develop in a similar way. Will there be such a thing as cannabis terroir? Absolutely. Will there be regional appellations, like "Bud du Winlaw"? I am quite sure. Will there be contests for best high? There already are. Will there be cannabis bus tours? There already are. Will there be pot pairings? No doubt, and hopefully they will go beyond Doritos. And will there be similar flowery and over-the-top product descriptions, like there are on the wine labels? No question. And I hope I get to write them.

12
PLACES OF ATTACHMENT

WE SEPARATE OURSELVES from nature in a thousand ways. Fortunately, there are devices for reversing that process. I did hit upon one such method, involving grasslands and a small metal frame.

Years ago, I was hired to make assessments of the impacts of cattle grazing on certain grasslands in BC's Southern Interior. To do this, I hired fencing contractors to build grazing exclosures, typically a hectare in size. Then my routine was to establish and monitor a set of permanent vegetation monitoring plots inside (ungrazed) and another set outside (grazed). Dry grasslands like ours change slowly, so every five years or so I would come back to remonitor the plots and review the differences. I did this for many years, in various parts of the Southern Interior. It was a job.

The coming-back part sounds pretty straightforward, but it isn't. My first challenge upon return was to locate the metal pins I had pounded to ground level to mark my plots. Relocating said pins five years later meant contending with poor memory, misplaced plot maps, and accumulation of dead plant litter, gopher mounds and cowpies. GPS units in those early days were only marginally helpful: their accuracy was within five metres in the hours between 11 a.m. and 2 p.m., but only when four or more satellites were in view.

My vegetation plots were miniature samples, tiny non-invasive slices, that attempted to represent the vegetation of an entire grazed landscape. In deciding where to locate plots, we researchers always face a certain dilemma: do we place them randomly, or do we trust our judgment enough to pick spots that are representative of the larger site under study? Time and available funds usually push us toward the latter.

Foresters have it easy. They identify the two or three tree species in their plot, count them, measure them and determine their age. We grassland ecologists are faced with dozens of species — lichens, mosses, grasses, broadleaf plants, shrubs and the occasional tree. We spend a lot of time on hands and knees, leafing through paper or digital plant taxonomy books.

There are three ways of monitoring grassland vegetation: frequency, biomass and cover. Counting individual plants — frequency — is rarely practical, since there can easily be a few hundred separate plants in a square metre. Clipping individual species, drying them and then weighing them to determine biomass yields great data, but the process is incredibly time-consuming. Most grassland work involves estimating cover: the amount of physical space that each species occupies within the boundaries of a defined plot.

The man who established the cover technique was Rexford Daubenmire, a prolific botanist who did extensive studies of the grasslands of Eastern Washington in the 1950s. His method was elegantly simple: he devised a rectangular rigid-wire frame that acts as a visual aperture. The frame, a tenth of a metre in size, sits on metal legs that hold it just above the top of the grass canopy. On your knees in front of the frame, you look down into it, identify each species within the rectangle, and then, taking the area of the frame as one hundred percent, estimate the percentage of the two-dimensional space occupied by each species. To generate a representative sample of the larger area under study, you do this many times, along linear transects. A typical arrangement is to lay out several twenty-five-metre transects and do a cover estimate at each metre point. The work then becomes a series of botanical genuflections, on twenty-five-metre pilgrimages. Each frame placement is, in effect, a "microplot," and when the data from all the microplots are averaged together, you have a lovely and imprecise approximation of the plant cover of a single grassland biome. Cover is a surrogate for biomass, and biomass is a surrogate for dominance. Knowing the dominant three or four species in an ecosystem helps us to characterize and label that ecosystem; knowing the full suite of species in that ecosystem helps us to flag the rare ones, and the invasives.

Daubenmire's optical frame method has stood the test of time because it is simple and repeatable. He chose the frame size based on the parameters of human eyesight: you can look down into a twenty-by-fifty-centimetre frame and see the entire space without having to move your head. The Daubenmire frame is cheap and can be made in any welding shop, and the legs can be removable. Another asset of the frame, important in Daubenmire's day: it fits nicely into a saddlebag.

Mine were not the first grazing exclosures in the BC Interior. I had the pleasure of remonitoring one north of Cranbrook that was built in 1952. In the 1960s, range scientists Alastair McLean and Edwin Tisdale tracked down two old exclosures, one near Merritt and the other near Kamloops, that were built in 1931. In an outstanding example of persistence and corporate memory, they monitored them in 1961 and again in 1968. I am still hoping to find information on an old exclosure near Riske Creek, in the Chilcotin country. It was built a century ago.

A single transect I got to visit, in Washington State's Okanogan County, was established in 1937. The original written directions to locate this one, in the Sinlahekin Valley, are as follows: "The transect lies between the two homesteads and is just south of the drift fence starting near a clump of chokecherry and running west through the bunchgrass." Truly, found poetry.

The study of nature is often confounded by "edge effects," where the chosen object or treatment is subtly influenced by some adjacent, but different, object or treatment. Such was the case with some of those early grazing exclosures: their small size meant that the data was confounded by edge effects. Back in the pre-drone days, I once strapped a small camera to a radio-controlled model airplane and flew it over one of my exclosures to get some low-level aerial shots. The photos revealed a narrow cattle trail, which I had not previously noticed, running all the way around the exclosure, just outside the fence. Perhaps the cows were attracted by greener grass inside the exclosure, but at any rate, they had certainly created an edge effect. I learned early on the value of large exclosures, and not to put any monitoring plots within ten metres of any fence line.

Grassland monitoring is best done at "peak phenology," the mid-May to late-June period when science and beauty come together. Most species are in flower then, which makes them easily identifiable. Often, I would be dealing with fifty or more higher plant species at an individual exclosure, not to mention the mosses and lichens. Intimate vegetative secrets and ecological phenomena were slowly revealed to me, on a five-year schedule. Of course, I looked for trends over time; that is what we scientists do. We replicate, we monitor, we analyze, and we look for longitudinal trends. Often, we have expectations — or more officially, hypotheses — about what should happen. More often, nature confounds those expectations, offering up instead its humbling complexity, randomness and annoying granularity.

My exclosures are all located well away from paved roads and towns, and the monitoring usually takes a full day or more. So it must have been the extended visits, plus a concentrated focus on the local vegetation, that fixed these places permanently in my mind. The plant cover data was the vestibule, but each of these two-hectare sites became small, grassed universes, unique unto themselves. The air, the insects, the shrub cover, the curiosity of the cows, the particular view when I stopped for a lunch break. The sense that I was taking the measure of an infinitesimally small but unique piece of the planet. An unexpected reacquaintance with an uncommon grass, or a tiny pussytoes. A pointed territorial reminder from a rattlesnake. The unconscious artistic placement of a rock, a sage and a balsamroot.

Over time, I came to terms with the knowledge that my data would simply gather electronic dust in some obscure government repository. I kept my own copies, though, and that, plus my affinity with these humble places, was satisfaction enough. It was no longer just a job.

Governments generally mean well, but they are not good custodians of long-term ecological monitoring data. Funding programs, staff and offices come and go, fiscal year-ends intervene, paper and digital records get lost or forgotten. A good alternative example is the discipline of ornithology, which is almost entirely driven by citizens, NGOs and universities. As one lifelong birder confided to me, "Our data is too important to be left in the hands of government agencies."

My human attachment to grasslands relates in a small way to a much larger animal attachment. Throughout the world, grasslands (also referred to as rangelands, or steppe) are associated with grazing mammals, but that statement hides some curious arithmetic. Mammals with hooves are called ungulates. Ungulates are divided by the number of hooves on each foot. Ungulates with one hoof (horses) or three hooves (rhinoceri) have simple stomachs. Ungulates with two hooves (cows, sheep, goats, antelope, bison, etc.) are ruminants. Ruminants have four stomachs and a bevy of gut microorganisms that help them digest dry grasses with high fibre content. So rangelands and their ruminants are intimately bound together. Every grassland seems to have its four-stomached companion, be it yak, zebra, bison or caribou, all except the grasslands of the intermountain West. This area, between the Rockies and the Cascades and including British Columbia's Southern Interior, is different. The reasons for this are speculative, infinitely debatable, and fascinating.

The curtain rises on a great North American grassland play. It takes place in an open-air Ice Age theatre, where monster grazers like the woolly mammoth and the superbison roam and feed. But their time onstage is brief. With the advance of the Holocene, they exeunt, likely due to declining habitat and Indigenous hunting pressure. Next act: the familiar plains bison finds the newly ice-free, warmer habitats of the Canadian Prairies and the US Great Plains much to its liking. Individual bison herd numbers grow to the thousands, and then to the tens of thousands as they roam these landscapes, consuming the grasses. The grasses, for their part, self-select and adapt to the intense grazing pressure. The surviving grasses are the rhizomatous or creeping-rooted types that keep their growing points down low, close to the ground or even under it. Some of the upright bunchgrass types also survive: these are species that can respond to grazing by rapidly producing new, lighter-weight leaves.

This same Pleistocene co-evolution play repeats itself, with other grazing animal actors, in the grasslands of Europe and on the steppes of Russia. But our intermountain grasslands, of southern BC and down through eastern Washington and Oregon, southern Idaho and northern Nevada, followed a totally different script. They became dominated by tall bunchgrasses — wheatgrasses and fescues — that have high growing points and thick, long-lived leaves. There are multiple factors behind this vast continental difference, but one stands out from all the rest: bison avoid narrow valleys.

Bison herds are always on the move, daily and seasonally. They favour landscapes with wide open vistas so they can detect human and animal predators from afar. Open landscapes favour the bison's twin defence mechanisms: massive herds and ferocious running speeds. The convoluted valleys and small open prairies of the intermountain West were not to their liking, and they avoided them. Other grazers such as antelope, elk, wild sheep and goats were present here, but only in minimal numbers and in very scattered locations.

The situation changed dramatically as cattle and horses moved northward into the Okanagan, on the heels of the Cariboo gold rush of the 1860s. In the ensuing rush of European settlement and the birth of BC's ranching industry, there was no awareness of this continental difference. Grass was grass — irrespective of species or location — there to be eaten by livestock. This was accepted fact in the minds of various grazing-based human communities around the world. Indeed, British Columbia's ranching industry was started by immigrants from the moist and forgiving grasslands of the British

Isles, where domestic cattle had been grazing for centuries. Little or no notice was taken as our native bunchgrasses began to fade and over time were largely replaced by invasive plants and the unpalatable sagebrush. There was always more cattle range over in the next valley.

Some of this ignorance is justifiable. Grasses are small, and damnably hard to tell apart. The average person immediately recognizes a forest as an ecosystem, but grasslands not so much. Grasslands are the Rodney Dangerfield of ecosystems: they get no respect.

It was not until the 1980s that range managers became aware of the fundamental difference between intermountain and prairie grasslands. "Evolution in Steppe with Few Large, Hooved Mammals," by Richard Mack and John Thompson, was quietly published in the *American Naturalist* journal, and the article has been resonating ever since. I love the title of this paper; it has great cadence, like *The Decline and Fall of the Roman Empire.* In the process of setting forth the thesis, the authors combine botany, geography, paleontology and anthropology. Not surprisingly, the paper refers to some of Rexford Daubenmire's earlier work on intermountain grasses. The authors go on to point out that this sensitivity to grazing has led to an ongoing replacement of intermountain native grasses by the invasive alien cheatgrass, a replacement that is far more extensive now than it was when the paper was first published, in 1982.

All of my exclosures have passed their twenty-year mark now; various plant species have waxed and waned, and the general trends I have identified are precious few. If grazing is eliminated, litter tends to build up, and more seed is set. After a decade of no grazing, the native bunchgrasses begin recovery, and some unexpected native wildflowers show up. Diffuse knapweed was once everywhere and is now hard to find due to successful insect biocontrol. Pocket gophers love deep grassland soils, and their fresh dirt mounds are magnets for weeds, both inside and outside exclosures. Much depends on individual site, season and grazing regime. Fire and

The Sky and the Patio

its absence is another profoundly important grassland element that must be considered. And possibly the near extinction of badgers, who once dined heartily on the pocket gophers.

Even though my job is long since over, my exclosures and I still reunite periodically, like old and trusted friends.

A young colleague of mine says the attachment to place begins with reciprocity. You give something to the land, and in return that land gives you an emotional bond or tie point. That tie point can be a space for mental retreat, cockeyed optimism, philosophical reflection or any one of a hundred other deeply personal feelings. This brings us back to William Jordan's eminently practical method for forging attachment to place, via ecological restoration. Performing physical work to restore damaged nature, with no expectation of material return, creates an enduring bond. In expanding on this notion, Jordan sees ecological restoration as a non-religious substitute for what churches have traditionally provided: a community of practice; a sense of collective shame as a prod to remedial action; and perhaps most importantly, reverence for an intangible that is beyond the self.

Long-term ecological monitoring (LTEM) became my personal nature-attachment device. Building a grazing exclosure, and then revisiting it every few years, is like going to a high-school reunion. The intervening years disappear as you encounter old friends. There is much more to LTEM than looking down into a Daubenmire frame. There are the joys of interpreting old field notes and relocating a previous researcher's monitoring plots; searching out old landscape photographs in museums and archives, discovering the exact location, and retaking the images; comparing old and new airphotos and counting rings on old fire-scarred trees. These are the tiny film clips we splice together, in an effort to restore a vast motion picture chronicling the internal progressions of nature and our human impacts upon them. LTEM and ecological restoration are like salmon and wine: they pair perfectly together.

Cattle and horses have definitely impacted our grasslands. Mine and many other exclosure studies show continuous grazing causes a general decrease in three benchmark native bunchgrasses: bluebunch wheatgrass, rough fescue and Idaho fescue. McLean and Tisdale proved the reverse: a prolonged period of no grazing allowed those bunchgrasses to come back. These productive and nutritious grasses, the ones that evolved with few large, hooved mammals, are highly sensitive to grazing, particularly during spring greenup. That spring growth period is critical, given the dry summers of the intermountain West.

Our native bunchgrasses, with their massive fibrous root systems, also store large amounts of atmospheric carbon deep in the soil. Can grazing reduction, reorganization or temporary elimination bring these grasses back? Have their ecological niches been permanently hijacked by invasive weeds? Can roading and ATV damage to grasslands be separated from cattle damage? What role does fire suppression play, in its slow conversion of grasslands into junk, wildfire-prone forests and sagelands? Are the results of disturbance reversible, or is ecological decline a one-way street? Are conservative, ecologically aware livestock grazing and grass-fed beef compatible with climate change mitigation?

My evening patio reading sometimes includes old field sheets and summaries from exclosure monitoring, to help chip away at these questions. Nerding out, if you will. It helps to glance up at that grassy western hillside now and then, to keep things in perspective.

13
CHINOOK WAWA

SPITLUM, **FOR THE** bitterroot plant. *Siya,* for the saskatoon. These nsyilxcən plant names, plus a few place names and salutations, have slipped into my everyday vocabulary. I hear nsyilxcən often, in invocations at the start of local events, as it is the traditional language of the Syilx peoples, otherwise known as the Okanagans. Nsyilxcən was spoken from Merritt east to Kaslo, and from Revelstoke south to Wenatchee. Many of our current place names, like Kelowna, Penticton, Keremeos and Osoyoos, are anglicized corruptions of nsyilxcən words. Indeed, the word *Okanagan* itself is a derivation. There is a nascent movement to repatriate some of these place names. The former Haynes Point Provincial Park near Osoyoos is now sẃiẃs Park, operated by the Osoyoos Indian Band. Other nsyilxcən words are beginning to appear up and down the Okanagan.

I would like to learn this language, which would be a challenge in itself, but there is an additional hurdle for the nsyilxcən learner: the orthography. For instance, this quotation:

> We, the Syilx Okanagan Peoples have spoken our nsyilxcən language since time immemorial, and we are responsible for the protection, revitalization and advancement of our nsyilxcən language.

translates to this, using the International Phonetic Alphabet:

> axaʔ iʔ kʷu syilx iʔ kʷu⁀sukʷnaqinx kʷu cnqilxʷcən ta nsyilxcən uɬ way t'əsxʷuy uɬ ta mnimɬtət kə ck'ɬqixʷstm

uɬ kə ctiɬstm, uɬ niʕip kə ck'ʷulmstm iʔ nsyilxcən aʔ nqilxʷcntət.

So my challenge is similar to what a Japanese or Arab immigrant faces when arriving in Canada: not only to learn new words, grammar, sentence structure and sounds, but a completely new orthography as well. While I continue to absorb bits and pieces of nsyilxcən (learning, for instance, that the upside-down e is pronounced like the e in *elephant*), I am attracted to another language: Chinook.

Chinook wawa, or Chinook-speak, is a hybrid, or pidgin language. Scholars say it is one of only two in all of North America, the other being Creole, spoken around New Orleans. Wawa's roots lie in Astoria, at the mouth of the Columbia River. This was the site of first prolonged contact between First Nations and white fur traders along the north Pacific coast, and Chinook developed as a trading language. Although Chinook did borrow from Chinookan, the local Indigenous language, whites struggled with certain Chinookan pronunciations, so many words were borrowed from the Nuuchahnulth (Nootka) language. Nuuchahnulth, spoken on the west coast of Vancouver Island, was more pronounceable by English tongues. French also became a contributing language, by way of wandering Québécois voyageurs. A number of English words were also folded in. Other words were borrowed from Algonquin and Hawaiian Kanaka, and, most mysteriously, a few words from the Japanese language. Chinook grammar is straightforward and utilitarian, and the nouns have no gender.

In the early 1800s, Chinook wawa spread rapidly up and down the coast, from Alaska to California, and then moved inland following major river systems: the Columbia, the Snake, the Fraser and the Thompson. Wawa is at its finest in describing tangible things like trade items, food, weather and geography.

We tend to forget how polyglot life was in and around BC in the early 1800s. In places like Kamloops, Prince George or Victoria, one could encounter Québécois voyageurs, Italian priests, Hawaiian labourers, Mexican drovers, Scottish second sons, Algonquian oarsmen, British traders, Nez Perce guides and even Japanese shipwreck survivors. Botanist David Douglas and geologist George Mercer Dawson, in their extensive travels around BC, found Chinook to be indispensable. Itinerant artist Paul Kane was familiar with the wawa. Susan Allison, an amazingly resilient English settler in the Similkameen, learned Chinook as a matter of course as she dealt with various First Nation groups up and down that valley. More recent users were anthropologist Franz Boas and BC artist Emily Carr. For a few brief decades, Chinook was British Columbia's lingua franca for travellers and traders, until it was eventually overtaken by English.

There is a host of Chinook geographical and place names throughout BC and the US Pacific Northwest, like Malakwa, Alki, Chumstik, Illlahee, Skookumchuk, Mowitch, Lolo, Siwash, Sitkum and Tyee. When I was a kid and would ask my dad where some particular town or place was located, his standard answer was "Oh, that's about halfway between Tillamook and Mukilteo." I trace my lifelong interest in geography back to that bombastic non-answer. *Skookum* is a Chinook word for "strong" or "powerful." *Skookumchuk* means "fast water." As teenage boys, we would refer to a particularly attractive girl as a skookumchick.

As I continue to absorb nsyilxcən words, I remind myself that it is just one of the thirty-odd Indigenous languages of British Columbia, and a three-hour drive in any direction would put me into a totally different linguistic homeland. So I am going to give Chinook a try. I like its broad geography, its rough-and-ready, street-level approach, and its openness to multicultural borrowing. I like the fact that no nation or ethnic group "owns" the language. If we resurrected Chinook, we could add useful words from languages that are now common in BC, like Spanish, Hindi and Mandarin. Wawa is said to have "limited grammar." For instance, the verb does not change based on the subject (e.g., we go, he go). This is another big plus for me, since grammar was never my strong suit.

Meanwhile, we British Columbians live with a host of British place names: Prince George, Princeton, Invermere, Britannia Beach and Ladysmith, to name just a few. I remember chatting with

The Sky and the Patio

long-time MLA Corky Evans about dropping all this musty British heritage stuff and changing the province's name to something else. His response: "Don, we need to wear the name *British Columbia* like a hair shirt."

I do have a Chinook-English dictionary, ready for patio perusal with a supper of fish and wine. Or rather, for my muckamuck, I will have pish and lum.

14
JOHANN WOLFGANG VON GOETHE AND THE BEE BALM

THIS BENCH SITS next to a native plant garden bordering the sidewalk across the street from Summerland's public library. I sit on it, preparing to follow the instructions of Johann Wolfgang von Goethe. Right next to the library is the auto parts store, and as I dither, I begin to distinguish a pattern in the cars that pull up and park in front of me. Drivers of big, late-model pickup trucks head for the auto parts store; owners of small, older SUVs and sedans tend to head for the library. This observation, however perceptive, is sheer procrastination. It postpones my assignment, given to us by Dr. Nancy Holmes, poet and professor, in a nature writing seminar at the library. She has given us paper instructions on the four steps of the Goethean method of nature observation, and sent us outside. Unfortunately, the relation between lifestyle and automobile choice falls outside the bounds of the assignment.

Goethe's first step is to choose a natural object for observation. Looking around, I fix on a group of anonymous, tall-stemmed plants near my bench. They are still in flower but are rather scruffy-looking, since it is late August. This sidewalk garden is nothing like wilderness or even nature, but it will let me practice the method from the comfort of my shady bench. For Step One, Goethe says to bracket and firmly set aside all foreknowledge — particularly the scientific — of the natural object being viewed, and see simply it as is. In this case, exact sense perception is easy since there isn't much to see. Tall-stemmed plants with occasional, slightly withered leaves. Round, spiky inflorescences with a few remaining pinkish

The Sky and the Patio

flowers, visited by a small bumblebee. I wondered, is this bee one of the astonishing 356 native bee species of the Okanagan? We are belatedly realizing these insects are far more aggressive pollinators than the introduced honeybee. I have heard that distinguishing one native bumblebee species from another requires detailed knowledge of their anal anatomy. Bumblebee proctology?

Oops. I snap another bracket around that diversionary scientific rabbit hole and get back to Goethe. Step Two is to observe the natural object passionately, visualize how it came into being, and allow the imagination free rein. Which is odd since Goethe was also a scientist. So I do that. My passionate observation of this group of plants is progressing well, but some vague sense of familiarity begins to hover in the suburbs of my consciousness, well beyond the brackets. I do know that I have limited control over a mental plant-identification engine that fires up whenever I step outside; it is one of the hazards of my profession. For this Goethean exercise, however, I have firmly shut the engine down. As I lean in for my passion-filled observation of these plants, a fact rips right through the thin fabric of my brackets: square stems. The stems of these plants are square in cross-section. The damnable autonomous plant ID motor restarts: square stems equals *Lamiaceae*, the mints. Absolutely diagnostic for the entire family. I pluck a leaf to sniff it: not quite mint, not quite lemon, but very pungent, like thyme or oregano. Right away, another autonomous mental motor starts up, this one of memory. Of midsummer Saskatchewan Prairie grasslands, of outrageously pink flowers among a green sea of native grasses. And that unique, unmistakable scent. Ignoring Goethe, the plant ID motor races to its conclusive finish line: *Monarda*. Yes. *Monarda fistulosa*. Bee balm, or wild bergamot.

What a lovely plant, named in honor of Nicholas Monardes (1493–1588), a Spanish doctor who studied herbal medicines brought back from the recently discovered New World. There are some twenty species within the Monarda genus, native to large parts of North America, but found only rarely in British Columbia. Ironically, it was the Europeans that popularized them as ornamentals. The name *bee balm* comes from the leaf's reputed ability to soothe bee stings, and the *wild bergamot* name comes from its scent similarity to the true citrus bergamot, a component of Earl Grey tea. Monarda flowers, with their long funnels and hanging lower lips, are hugely popular with insect pollinators, but the leaves are not. In fact, Indigenous peoples of the prairies used a monarda leaf concoction to keep their meat from spoiling. Reviewing contemporary herbalism literature, bergamot oil seems to be a cure for pretty much everything from warts to menstrual cramps, making this skeptic a bit suspicious. Monarda was traditionally wild-harvested on the Canadian Prairies and sold to perfume makers, who used the essential oil as a base ingredient in their products. That cottage industry disappeared when chemists were able to synthesize a laboratory replacement for the oil. Progress of a sort.

Okay, enough of all that. Bracket all that historical, economic and scientific stuff and put it aside. Goethe's Step Three: stop telling this plant what *it* is and give *it* a chance to explain itself *to you* — to all your senses, and to your imagination. Turn off your woo-woo shit detector, trust Goethe, and seek new organs of perception.

I, Monarda, arise on foreign ground, miles and generations from my prairie origins. Reaching up, yearning for sunlight, for pollination, for recognition. I did not fashion my scent for you, but perhaps it will aid in my quest for recognition, for standing. I have passed through many unknown hands and soils. I have been selected over my sisters, for the way my stamens hang, or perhaps it was my particular shade of pink. I was reproduced in a greenhouse, far from my shortgrass prairie roots. As I struggle to express myself to this uncouth, bearded observer, I compete for his attentions with women in summer clothing who stroll the sidewalk beside us.

Step Four: transcend the particular organism and merge with its archetype. One of Goethe's poems illustrates this:

The Sky and the Patio

The infinite freedom of the growing leaf.

As I shuffle my Goethe instructions, one page falls to the sidewalk. A young woman in tight jeans with a hunting knife strapped to her belt picks it up and reads it. "This is really cool," she enthuses. "Can I keep it?" Of course, I agree, sensing a potential convert to passionate observation, but now I am missing Step Four. No problem. I get the gist of the method. Bracket all the foreknowledge and all the assumptions. Do Not Pass Go and proceed directly to passionate observation. Integrating all that rational stuff can come later. And if Goethe could do this, with his simultaneous careers as poet, playwright, novelist, scientist, statesman, theatre director, critic and amateur artist, surely I can too.

15
THE SINGULARITY OF FRIVOLOUS PURPOSE

THIS GRANDFATHER SHRUB has stiff, arching branches, tiny grey-green leaves, and a massive, twisted trunk. It is so sprawling that I can't get close enough to accurately measure its height. From the perimeter, adding my two metres and eyeballing the topmost branch, I guess it at close to four metres tall. Definitely old-growth for a dryland shrub that typically matures at waist height. God knows what this one has been through in its many decades of life. The weathered trunk has strips of papery bark hanging from it, like medals on an old soldier. The shrub's multitude of branches are a chaotic mix of live and dead, upright and drooping. The whole plant occupies a footprint the size of a living room.

I stand beside this ancient antelope bitterbrush for some time, for no obvious reason. Its tiny leaflets are fleshy, and their tips are indented, giving the impression of three stubby fingers. The shrub is a preferred browse species for wild ungulates, as well as a source of traditional medicines. In solidarity I chew a leaf: it is crunchy and starchy at the same time. The bitter taste does come through, but it is mild.

Uncommon here in the South Okanagan, this shrub connects me to a vast stretch of western American geography, where it is quite common and even dominant in some areas. For some obscure reason, antelope bitterbrush the *plant* is only yellow-listed in British Columbia's endangered species ranking, but the *plant community* — antelope bitterbrush together with needleandthreadgrass — is red-listed.

There are several barriers to the recognition I believe this complex plant deserves. On casual glance, it has a damnable resemblance to another dryland shrub — sagebrush. And then there is the problem with the name, which is variously antelope bitterbrush, antelopebrush, bitterbrush, greasewood, black sage, quininebrush, Purshia or *Purshia tridentata*. This is not helpful. Reluctantly, I will go with the name antelopebrush, even though there is no record of any pronghorn antelope ever setting a hoof in British Columbia. Furthermore, that fleet and lovely beast is not an antelope at all.

I have known this shrub casually for many years, but a new compulsion of unknown origin urges me toward a deep dive into this plant, and to map its distribution in our Okanagan valley. As I stand beside my veteran, I know it is close to the very ragged northern edge of its entire continental range. E-Flora BC, the University of British Columbia's comprehensive online encyclopedia of BC plants, contains a map showing twelve documented antelopebrush locations in the valley, the earliest dating back to 1959. The observer names attached to each location read like a who's who of prominent BC botanist elders: Cannings, Ceska, Demarchi, Pavlick, Scotter. That should mean something.

Most of the E-Flora antelopebrush map dots are congregated around Osoyoos, hard by the American border. And indeed, panning down south of the border on E-Flora's map, Eastern Washington has dozens of antelopebrush dots. Two of the Canadian dots are located up on Anarchist Mountain, just east of Osoyoos, but one of them is obviously misplaced, speaking to the difficulty of properly recording (and digitizing) lats, longs, UTMs and declinations. Moving northward up the Okanagan, there is an outlier dot in the mountains west of Oliver, which is odd since antelopebrush is mostly a valley-bottom species. The most northerly dot is near Oyama, a small community north of Kelowna. This one was identified by Dr. George Scotter in 2015, and his note says, "This is likely the northern limit of *Purshia tridentata* in the Okanagan." That note should also contribute to standing, as Dr. Scotter was one of Canada's foremost conservationists.

Curiously, there is no antelopebrush in the adjacent Lower Similkameen Valley, an area of very similar climate and soils to the South Okanagan. There is a Syilx story that explains that absence.

A dot on the E-Flora map is just that. It represents the location where the species was collected and subsequently dried, mounted, labelled, externally verified, and submitted to the University Herbarium, which finally uploads its data to E-Flora. If you do a search for a common species on E-Flora, like dandelion, you will get eighty dots. (If BC homeowners contributed dandelion locations, there would be a trillion dots.) With eighty plant dots, you can easily draw in the sensuous curves of a species distribution map, extrapolating the short distances between adjacent dots. And voila, you have just abstracted a component of nature and placed it elegantly into a defined, two-dimensional, distributional space. But with only twelve dots, you can't make a map of our Okanagan antelopebrush distribution. The shrub suffers the indignity of being uncommon but not rare. Or perhaps just ignored.

I have compiled a few unofficial sightings myself. The Nk'Mip Desert Cultural Centre and the Osoyoos Desert Centre both host stands of antelopebrush, as does the Nature Trust property just north of the community of Gallagher Lake. The veteran I describe stands proudly on an isolated and thoughtful hillside east of Penticton. There are fourteen individuals in a strip along the old Kettle Valley Railway route, near Trout Creek. And I have found a few tucked in among the endless suburbs and strip malls in the town of Westbank.

An unofficial antelopebrush transplant has been growing in our Summerland front yard for a decade. This particular individual's place of origin was a highway road allowance outside of Osoyoos. Because the soil there was sandy, I was able to dig deeply, capturing most of the root system and the soil surrounding it. That probably contributed to the success of my transplant. This was a transgression, but a calculated one. I knew sooner or later the road

The Sky and the Patio

allowance would be sprayed or mowed, or the highway would be widened. The shrub is now an icon in our yard, and may someday reach living-room size as well. Its rough texture suggests wildness and drought, so different from the lush and manicured vegetation of our neighbourhood. As much as I love this plant, it will never appear on my Okanagan distribution map.

George Mercer Dawson weighed in on the challenges of mapping plants in this province:

> With [British Columbia's] diversified and bold physical features, the lines indicating the geographical range of the various species of plants do not assume in it the broad rounded forms found in less mountainous districts. The peculiarities in distribution while adding interest to the study, renders an intimate knowledge of the topography of the country an essential prerequisite to its prosecution.

Amen, George. You said a mouthful.

To become familiar with antelopebrush in the Okanagan, one also becomes familiar with trespass. Many times, I have gone up some side road, headed for a hillside dotted with the distinctive dark clumps which, by binoculars, I know to be antelopebrush, only to find locked gates and No Trespassing signs. In between me and my hillside destination are exclusive designer homes and boutique vineyards. In my quest, I have done my share of explaining to concerned landowners. Reciting the common law that says private landowners cannot block access to the Queen's land generally falls on unsympathetic ears.

Antelopebrush flowers require cross pollination, which is mostly done by insects. The small, pear-shaped seeds are heavy, tending to fall straight down to the ground upon maturity. This is a problem, since antelopebrush shrubs don't start producing seed until they are large and mature, leaving little room for new seedlings to establish themselves underneath their parent plant. Enter the rodents. Every fall, mice, chipmunks and squirrels collect the seeds, husk them, and bury them in little caches here and there, as winter provisions. Fortunately for the shrub, these busy rodents either cache way more than they can ever eat, or else they suffer from poor spatial memory. The sprouting of seedlings from unopened rodent seed caches is the primary means of antelopebrush stand regeneration. Not only do the rodents actually plant the seeds by burying them, they dramatically speed up the germination process by husking them.

A few antelopebrush genotypes also have the ability to "layer," meaning their lower branches droop all the way to the ground and then root in place, eventually creating a new plant.

How old is an old antelopebrush? Some American reports put veterans at over 100 years, one specimen as old as 160 years. Out of curiosity, I took home a dead stem from one of our local populations, cross-sectioned it and sanded it smooth. In spite of the stem's irregular, twisted shape, full of indentations and wrap-arounds, its annual growth rings showed up quite clearly under a magnifying glass. This particular sample, about 3.5 inches (9 centimetres) across at the widest point, was thirty-five years old. So now I have a rough proxy for shrub age in the form of stem diameter.

I take pleasure in reading obscure scientific literature, and there is a remarkably large amount of published research on antelopebrush, nearly all of it from the United States. It turns out this plant, along with a few other dryland shrubs, has adopted the strategy of the legumes. Like peas, beans, alfalfa and clover, antelopebrush hosts a microbe that can take nitrogen gas directly from the air and convert it to plant-available nitrate nitrogen. Quite a trick, if you think about it. The microbe responsible, which lives in tiny nodules on the roots, is referred to as an "actinomycete microsymbiont." What obscure and fascinating scientific worlds reside behind those two words.

The research literature defines antelopebrush as a "climax" species, but then turns right around and says it is also a pioneer colonizer of recently burned areas.

The Sky and the Patio

Dr. Sylvie Desjardins was studying the Behr's hairstreak, a federally endangered butterfly that is an "antelopebrush obligate," meaning that it requires antelopebrush to complete its life cycle. The diminutive hairstreak is a dull grey until it opens its wings to expose colours ranging from orange to bronze. Dr. Desjardins and her associates were doing butterfly mark-recapture work in the antelopebrush stand near Gallagher Lake when they noticed activity in a nearby ponderosa pine. Dozens of hairstreaks emerged from the tree and began a tumbling, vertical dance in the air adjacent to the pine, creating a kind of butterfly conveyor belt. I am sure there is some tested and replicated scientific hypothesis that explains this curious behaviour. I must see that research, but at the same time I demand equal time for the frivolous, the spiritual and the artistic explanations of that dance as well. Science and art are, in fact, consenting adults.

As if the antelopebrush ecological stage were not crowded enough, now the ants come marching in. Researchers find that ants remove external parasites from hairstreak caterpillars in exchange for tiny droplets of a delectable (to ants, anyway) amino acid the caterpillars produce. Imagine an antelopebrush day spa for hairstreak larvae.

The ponderosa pine, the antelopebrush and the Behr's hairstreak have an uneasy communal relationship with fire. Hairstreaks prefer veteran, not juvenile, ponderosas for overnight roosting, but it is hard to produce veteran ponderosas without periodic fire. The hairstreaks also prefer old-growth antelopebrush — thirty years old or more — to lay their eggs on, and a thirty-year old antelopebrush is quite likely to die in a fire, due to the accumulation of dead, flammable branches around its base. Further complicating matters, if fire has been absent or suppressed for a long time, pine needles accumulate on the ground, which deters rodents from caching antelopebrush seeds. And the slow accumulation of new trees as a result of fire suppression means the eventual loss of antelopebrush, which needs full sunlight. A complex web they do weave, these organisms.

The Singularity of Frivolous Purpose

My friend and colleague Dr. Dennis St. John, a butterfly expert, complains that the hairstreak gets all the press while another endangered antelopebrush obligate, the Nuttall's sheepmoth, languishes in obscurity. The hummingbird-sized sheepmoth is a true work of pop art: its wing patterns would be right at home in a modern art gallery.

Traditional botany — identifying plants and mapping their distribution — is laborious enough, but identifying and mapping *plant communities* is hugely challenging. Just when you think you have pinned down two representative species that typically cohabitate, and you've come up with a nice catchy name — like *Idaho fescue-snowberry* — nature throws you a curve and you find the two species in widely separated locations. Or a fellow plant nerd will take issue with your pairing. Botanists tend to be an argumentative bunch, and vague concepts like plant communities provide glorious opportunity for debate.

As part of my deep dive, I consulted the BC Species and Ecosystems Explorer, which contains fifty-four mapped polygons of the antelope bitterbrush/needleandthreadgrass ecological community, ranging from the US border at Osoyoos, northward to the town of Kaleden. This mapping process differs from E-Flora BC's in two ways: it locates a broader ecological community rather than a single plant species, and it provides an estimate of the areal extent of the community. True to form, however, each mapped location comes with a lengthy list of caveats.

Not satisfied with plant or plant-community level of mapping, I am also looking to the biome level, which defines a multiple flora *and* fauna community, thus upping the debate ante considerably.

The vast interior of Western North America, between the Rockies and the coastal ranges, extending from the BC Southern Interior down into the high plains of Colorado and Wyoming and as far south as New Mexico, is dry. Generally hot summers and cold winters, but overall, mostly dry. Drought-tolerant grasslands and shrublands cover the lower basins and valleys; tough, sparse trees like ponderosa pine and juniper take to the hillsides. Flowering plants tend to be small and not showy; many compress their reproductive cycle into early spring. Reptiles are common. Except for the mesic grassland areas, soils tend to be coarse, often sandy, some just a thin veneer over bedrock. Organic matter content is generally low. This biome contains many closed water basins. The classic is the great basin of Salt Lake, but there are many other smaller, saline depressions with no external drainage. Our own White Lake basin near Kaleden is one such example.

The southern boundary of this hypothetical biome lies somewhere around the Mexican border. The northern boundary? Well, that is where it gets interesting. What are the iconic species of this biome, the ones that could collectively define its borders? Ponderosa pine is certainly one. As much as I would like to put antelopebrush forward, it is secondary to its compatriot, Wyoming big sagebrush, *Artemisia tridentata*, found in every corner of the biome. An iconic large mammal? Perhaps bighorn sheep. A reptile? Surely the western diamondback rattlesnake. What to call this vast piece of real estate? One could revert to purely physiographic descriptions, combining the Columbia Plateau with the Basin and Range Province, but that leaves little room for ecological inspiration. How about the Intermountain Biome, or the Sagebrush Biome, or the Great Basin Biome? Occasionally, I see the South Okanagan referred to as "Canada's pocket desert" or "the northern end of the Sonoran Desert." That is simple tourism and realtor hyperbole. To qualify as an official desert, no more than 250 millimetres of annual precipitation may fall upon you. Osoyoos, the driest town in the Okanagan, gets 300.

The Great Basin Biome is probably the least inaccurate name on the list. No matter which name is chosen, it will provoke endless discussion. But the fact remains that there is a host of common American intermountain plant and animal species whose very northern distribution ends somewhere around the BC towns of Keremeos or Oliver, with a few extending up as far as Vernon. Which is to say, this South Okanagan–Similkameen of mine shares a broad ecological kinship with places like Yakima, Washington; Twin

Falls, Idaho; Sweet Grass, Montana; Burns, Oregon; Winnemucca, Nevada; Sweetwater, Wyoming; Rio Blanco, Colorado; Ogden, Utah; and Flagstaff, Arizona.

Why should we care that the antelopebrush, the rattlesnake, the yellow-breasted chat, the Grand Coulee owl clover, the badger and thirty or so other species are at the absolute far northern end of their geographical range here, and are consequently deemed rare in BC, when they are in fact common to the south of us? After all, these species are rare not by biology, but by arbitrary forty-ninth parallel geopolitics ("politically peripheral species," according to one wag). I am so glad you asked that question, and I have two answers for it.

Any North American plant or animal living at the northern edge of its geographical range has to be adaptable, since it copes with far more climatic and nutritional uncertainty than those living in the centre or southern regions. As a result, northern populations possess more diverse genetics than their southern compatriots. They come from the deep end of the gene pool, so to speak. A diverse gene pool is a tremendously valuable asset; it makes a species more adaptable to new situations.

The second reason is a painfully obvious one: climate change. As our climate warms and the summer season lengthens, some current local species will either move northward or upward, become scarce, or drop out entirely. "Nature abhors a vacuum" is a trite phrase, but it certainly applies here. The ecological niche left by the maladapted native species will be filled by another, better adapted species. These better-adapted species will come from one of two ecological warehouses. One warehouse consists of invasives, which are typically aggressive, have high reproductive rates and thrive on disturbance. The other warehouse, of native species, lies in the Great Basin (or Sagebrush or Intermountain, etc. etc.) biome to the south of us. A plant whose current northern distribution ends at, say, Yakima, or a lizard that does not venture beyond Omak, will in a very short time be comfortable in the climate of Oliver and Penticton. By extension, some of our vacated Okanagan native species will become comfortable in Williams Lake and Quesnel.

The northward migration of newly adapted native species is absolutely contingent on ecological connectivity, a concept simple to understand but tremendously difficult to implement. Providing relatively continuous northward terrestrial, riparian and aquatic corridors through the Okanagan requires a fundamental change in urban and land use planning. This valley is the most direct route between the Great Basin Biome and the vast Central Interior of BC, but it is the very narrow and highly fragmented neck of a continental hourglass. I hope we are up to this land management challenge.

But back to mapping. It is a curious exercise. A map or a satellite image is nature vastly reduced, simplified and two-dimensionalized. A map or satphoto makes the landscape accessible from an armchair. Mapping a coastline or a national border is straightforward; since there are defined edges, you make very few assumptions. But to map plant distribution, you either leave it as an uninspired series of dots or you decide on a minimum threshold of plant density per hectare or some such heinous measure, so you can daringly draw a continuous line between what is in and what is out. In the case of mapping a plant community, ecosystem or biome, you overlap data from several species to draw your consensual map. In either case, you have to consider the outliers, the little pockets of your chosen species that are remote from the main distribution. Are they a case of mistaken identification? Did someone plant them there? Are they insignificant anomalies that can safely be ignored? Are they remnants of past distribution, or a harbinger of things to come?

For antelopebrush, I started with a map generated by Ted Lea that shows the present and historical distribution of the antelopebrush/needleandthreadgrass plant community in the South Okanagan. Ted did this by "backcasting," first mapping distribution on contemporary airphotos, then mapping again on archival airphotos from the 1940s. By measuring the change over that time span, he projected back to the original, pre-settlement extent. His data is sobering: from 1860 to 2000, there was a sixty percent loss of this plant community. And the beat since the millennium goes on, as this valley accumulates vineyards, spaghetti suburbs, prisons, racetracks, big-box stores and strip malls.

Even putting aside the massive and obvious losses to development, antelopebrush distribution is still quirky and unpredictable. As I began to pay close attention to this plant, I could see dominant stands of antelopebrush on one portion of a hillside, and none on another. All this rubbernecking was putting me at risk, so I decided to stop scanning while driving on Highway 97 and save the windshield botany for side roads.

Next, I turned to soil mapping, a very detailed but rarely consulted layer of Valley data. Doing some rough correlations between known antelopebrush locations and the respective soil textures, I found them growing on loamy sand, gravelly sandy loam, sandy loam and silt loam. But they totally avoided the very fine-textured silt soils found in certain areas along the valley bottom.

Antelopebrush likes its soils warm, coarse and deep. So do wineries. It is an unfair contest.

Soils, housing developments and vineyards explain a portion of antelopebrush's discontinuity, but fire can account for another. Decadent stands with lots of fuel accumulation can be killed in a hot wildfire, leaving little or no regeneration. This could explain some of the abrupt and arbitrary boundaries I see on the hillsides, but not all. Other mechanisms are at work.

The E-Flora antelopebrush marker in Fairview, west of the town of Oliver, stood out for me, more as a question mark than a dot. The shrub's elevation range in the valley is typically between 350 to 450 metres above sea level, and Fairview is a mountainous side valley at some 600 metres. So I went to investigate, and discovered a large antelopebrush population there. The area was treeless, but there was abundant evidence of a previous wildfire, in the form of burnt snags and tree stumps. Returning home, I burrowed into another favourite internet haunt, the BC government's IMAPBC website, to look at wildfire history in the area. Sure enough, the map polygon of wildfire number KA0805, which occurred in 1969, closely matched the extent of the Fairview antelopebrush population. Dennis St. John, a fountain of Okanagan knowledge, alerted me to another isolated population east of Oliver, far above the rest at 800 metres. Not surprisingly, IMAPBC recorded a fire there as well, in 1975. Both of these wildfires must have been cool, low-intensity types, allowing some shrubs to survive and then propagate.

Fire has multiple levels of severity, and antelopebrush has varying responses to fire severity. The two together amount to a quandary on top of a paradox.

Then there is the anomaly of the shrub's presence in BC's Rocky Mountain Trench, a higher, colder valley than the Okanagan. Or the fact that in Eastern Washington it commonly mingles with big sagebrush, but never does in BC.

The first mention I have found for antelopebrush in the Okanagan is from the journals of that indefatigable traveller, George Mercer Dawson. This is how he describes the country to the north of present-day Osoyoos: "The valley a huge wide flat bottomed trough, with no timber, scanty bunch grass &c. & open thickets of ragged looking 'Chaparaal' giving it a weird & strange aspect."

Here, Dawson refers to antelopebrush using the borrowed Spanish term *chaparral*, which originally described the shrub landscapes of Spain, Mexico and Southern California.

The *tridentata* part of the shrub's scientific name made sense to me, but the origin of the genus name, *Purshia,* kept gnawing at my curiosity until I looked it up. Frederick Pursh (1774–1820), a young German botanist recently emigrated to Philadelphia, was working for Benjamin Smith Barton, an eminent doctor, philosopher, botanist and egomaniac. Lewis and Clark had just returned from their famous expedition, and on Thomas Jefferson's recommendation they entrusted their entire dried plant collection to Barton, to identify and catalogue. Barton was too busy advancing his credentials in various fields, so the work devolved to humble young Frederick. Among the samples was an unknown shrub that William Clark had collected as the expedition travelled along the Blackfoot River in northwestern Montana. Pursh named the shrub

Tigarea tridentata. The word *Tigarea* is barbarous, meaning it has no meaning (other than "cigar" in Romanian). After finishing the Lewis and Clark work, Pursh moved to Montreal to undertake a flora of Canada. Pursh's entire collection burned in a fire and he died a penniless alcoholic at age forty-six. The botanical community posthumously renamed the shrub *Purshia*, in his honour. Botany certainly has its share of human drama.

In one antelopebrush research paper, the author called the shrub a post-Pleistocene relic, implying that it does not fit in this modern climatic era. I refuse to accept that, and instead see it as an ecological elder, a holder of vast post-Pleistocene wisdom. The Syilx people have their own stories about antelopebrush; we honkies have virtually none, and we need them. The only one I could find was written by local settler Isabel MacNaughton in the 1940s, which was actually adapted from an original Syilx story. Here is a snippet:

> Greasewoods carry cheer enough
> To brighten all the hill.
> Greasewood bloom is neat and gay
> Like elf-lamps burning high,
> Like little yellow candle-wicks
> Alight against the sky.

As a settler seeking my own nature bonds, I wonder if antelopebrush could become my spirit creature. It would fit nicely with my emerging philosophy of Honky Agnostic Land-Based Mysticism. I can envision my spirit ceremony; it would happen on a solstice. I would first perform a preparatory sauna cleanse at Penticton's recreation centre, and then I would proceed to a thoughtful hillside, together with senior botanists, aging hippies, and the Spirit of the West. The back of my ceremonial motorcycle jacket would be embroidered with antelopebrush images: the shrub in profile, a three-fingered leaf, the western harvest mouse, a pear-shaped seed, a flame, a hairstreak and a root nodule. As the ceremony concludes,

The Sky and the Patio

a sacrificial bough of antelopebrush is laid across my outstretched forearms. I am more than half-serious about this.

This ancient antelopebrush I stand next to has been waiting patiently in order to speak its piece. Engage with me, it says. Unlock my ecological secrets. Stand with me, write my stories, and give me standing. In return, I will be the patient recipient of your confused honky settler yearnings. Together, we will abide.

16
THE ENDURING PLEASURES OF THE WOODSTOVE

EVERY FALL, THERE comes a time when evening patio meals come to an end, and more of daily life moves reluctantly indoors. But a compensating pleasure awaits: the woodstove and the rituals that accompany it. Our stove comes from a foundry on Vancouver Island, and somehow it combines both sturdiness and elegance. Its squat, wide firebox and curved iron legs remind me of a bulldog, but at the same time the proportions and detailing speak of classical aesthetics. Of course, we have the two obligatory bi-metal, heat-driven fans sitting on top of the stove. The air movement they create is minimal, but the tiny amount of free energy, courtesy of the Peltier effect, appeals to us. The woodstove sits on a raised, tiled platform we built, which is just the right height for sitting beside the stove while pretending to mind the fire. The firebox door has a tempered-glass window that provides a compelling view of the fire inside. God knows for how long we humans have been staring at evening fires.

When my wife sits on the platform by the stove with a glass of wine in her hand and our little longhaired dachshund dog asleep on her lap, I do feel a bit superfluous.

The woodstove cycle starts in March, when local cherry and apple trees are pruned. Orchardists often welcome scroungers like me who save them the trouble of collecting the prunings off the ground. A bit later on in the spring, I do my own backyard pruning. Branches too thick to be cut up for compost become kindling.

The next phase of the cycle starts on a midsummer day about twenty kilometres out of town, in a dirt-bike sacrifice area that is full of stagnated, peckerpole ponderosa pine trees. Rather than cutting up mature trees and splitting the wood, I opt for smaller candidates that measure five or six inches in diameter. The resulting firewood has less BTU equivalent than older, denser wood, but it saves me the splitting, and it takes one more tree from this former open grassland that is now burdened with far too many. A key element of this phase of the woodstove cycle is a working chainsaw, and mine can be quite temperamental. If I have to pull the starter rope more than half a dozen times, my shoulder joint complains bitterly for days afterward. Occasionally, I can snag one of my sons to go on firewood forays with me, and I let him do the saw work while I load the cut wood into the back of our ancient Ford Explorer. Fortunately, the sons also understand chainsaw-sharpening, an arcane art I have never mastered.

My woodstove cycle also includes invasives. The tree of heaven (*Ailanthus altissima*), one of the world's most inappropriately named species, is a Chinese invader that is rapidly colonizing the Okanagan's riparian zones. I did some volunteer time cutting them down with the chainsaw. Looking at the growth rings, I was struck by how fast they grow, and how badly they smell. One of the tree's unofficial names is "stinking sumac." (Another is "the tree from hell.") Given the two qualities of fast growth and stench, I assumed the tree would make terrible firewood, but greed triumphed and I took a load home anyway. It turned out the smell dissipates as the wood dries, and the firewood quality is acceptable. So now I tell everyone it is open season on the tree of heaven, but cutting one down does trigger a raft of new sprouts around the cut stump, so be prepared for a long battle.

Next in the woodstove cycle comes firewood stacking, one that brings with it a fundamental contradiction: the driest, most burnable wood is always at the bottom of your pile. Short of an elaborate series of shelves or a conveyor belt of some kind, there seems no way to resolve this paradox. Our woodpile is against the west-facing wall of a toolshed; I have put in vertical wooden uprights so it is divided into sections, making a kind of firewood library. With this arrangement I can sometimes skirt the paradox by putting freshly cut wood in its own section, rather than piling it on top of older wood.

The apple and cherry wood that we scrounge are delightfully hard, long-burning woods, but stacking them is a challenge. Both species get heavily pruned, so the resulting firewood is lumpy, curvy, knotty and very difficult to stack. But well worth the trouble.

Very occasionally, a mature orchard gets ripped out, when the farmer replants with a newer variety or switches to wine grapes. That presents the rare opportunity to go from forearm-sized prunings to full tree trunks, the diameter of telephone poles. Once these are cut into woodstove-length rounds and seasoned for a while, the next chore is to split them. With ponderosa pine, a good heavy axe is all you need. Not so with cherry and apple. For these two, you need a sledgehammer, an iron splitting wedge, and a primitive, pugilistic desire to prevail. These hardwoods fight back. Deeper and deeper the wedge goes into the wood, as your sledgehammer blows become more forceful and precise, but nothing happens. There is no welcome splitting sound and sight of bright heartwood, as unity becomes duality. Your sledgehammer work shifts from pugilistic to reptilian, your shoulders are going to be sore for a week, but nothing matters now except victory. A few more apocalyptic blows and the wedge is now so deeply and firmly embedded in the round that you can't hit it with the sledge anymore. All-out war suddenly grinds to a halt. This round has imprisoned your iron wedge, and is laughing at you. Only then do you discover a fundamental axiom of splitting apple and cherry wood: thou must have a second wedge on emergency standby, which you can use to liberate its brethren.

Fire contained within a woodstove is a live and sentient presence. It moves and breathes and rages and dies. Fire is remarkably random: I am conscious of that every time I create the initial nest of crumpled newspaper and kindling. I can never predict where the flames will catch, if they catch at all. There is always that moment of tension just after light-up. Will my choice of paper, the degree of crumpling, the diameter and dryness of the kindling, and the architecture of my ignition structure bring a fire to life or cause it to expire, forcing a quick resuscitation with the trusty bellows? Timing is also important. If I am in a rush and try to hurry a new fire by placing larger-diameter wood over the kindling too soon, I kill it. Then there is the question of the draft. Closing the damper a notch or two can either smother a fire or enhance it. As the fire matures, banking the embers close together prolongs it. Somehow, these responses are all very lifelike.

    I have one of those butane fireplace lighters, but much prefer striking a match. That is a curious phrase, "striking a match." As writer Nicholson Baker rightly points out, we scratch matches, we don't strike them. Ideally, I would use a flint and steel, paying homage to my Irish and Norwegian ancestors. Our bellows hangs on the wall next to the woodstove. It is an essential implement if the kindling is too thick or not quite dry. If the crumpled paper loses its flame and is reduced to embers, bellows can come to the rescue. Randomness operates here as well: twenty bellow strokes in one spot can have no effect, but two or three strokes in another random spot and flames suddenly reappear. Bellows must have been a staggeringly important invention back in ancient times, when someone first stitched up a bag of animal skin and put a nozzle on one end.

    Beyond the kindling stage, the fire is in a state of either open flame or glowing embers, and there seems to be an incredibly delicate balance between the two. I can put a fresh log onto a pile of red-hot embers and — nothing happens. The embers continue to glow, wisps of steam might issue from the log, but all is quiet in the firebox. This condition might persist for half an hour, or maybe all evening. But then I can add a tiny piece of dry kindling or one puff with the bellows and voila! Active flame. In doing this I make no significant changes to conditions within the firebox; I simply add a minute catalyst, a trigger, that causes the fire to change state.

Glowing embers may generate as much heat as open flames, but they are far less entertaining.

This unpredictable near-organism behind the stove's tempered-glass window connects me, in miniature, to fire behaviour, the role of fire on the landscape, and to wildland firefighting. The same randomness I see in my firebox is writ large across dry forest landscapes: it is profoundly difficult to predict where and when wildfires will start, and how they will behave. Wildland firefighters do, however, have one very consistent predictor of fire behaviour: the 30:30:30 rule. When air temperatures are above thirty degrees centigrade, ambient humidity is at less than thirty percent, and windspeeds are over thirty kilometres an hour, wildfires become extremely dangerous and nearly impossible to fight.

The fire expert Stephen Pyne describes how the physical scale of fire has made it particularly useful to humans over time. If we were the size of elephants, fire would be useless, and if we were the size of ants, it would be terrifying. However, this scale advantage is changing, as wildfires get bigger and more intense. Pyne suggests we may have already passed through the Anthropocene era and are now entering the Pyrocene.

The public's view of wildland fire is created by lurid clips on evening TV news; fires are seen as an alien monster or an act of God, one that fortunately happens somewhere else and not in our own hometown. This view obscures the emerging discipline of fire science. As random as fire is, we now have detailed parameters characterizing aerial and ground fuels, fire weather, fire return intervals and fire itself. Our fire scientists and firefighters are comfortable with terms like *energy release component, 100-hour fuel moisture* and *burn index*. They grapple not only with the enormous task of controlling our current climate-enhanced wildfires, but also with how to reduce fuel loading to lessen the severity of future wildfires.

The dance of flames in our living room woodstove reminds me of the nude wrestling match between Alan Bates and Oliver Reed in the 1969 film *Women in Love*, which also took place in a living room, although one far larger and more ornate than ours. The scene was extravagant, arresting and sexually ambiguous. The action was made all the more potent because it took place in front of a roaring fire in the room's enormous fireplace. I went to see the film because of Stanley Kauffman, who reviewed pretty much every movie, including this one, from 1958 to 2013. In a youthful but failed attempt at becoming an intellectual, I read highbrow magazines, and that was how I found Kauffmann. His writing stood out as he reviewed the groundbreaking movies of the 1960s. Somehow, the man was able to stay current with the rapidly changing zeitgeist of movies for some five decades, revelling in pure cinematic enjoyment but simultaneously diving deep into acting and plot. Stanley Kauffmann wrote his last movie review at age ninety-five, perhaps in front of a fireplace.

Our woodstove saves us a few dollars in heating costs every winter month, but its real value is as a provider of daily rituals, of connections to nature, and of creature comforts. Another such provider is the bathtub: ours is large enough that I can immerse most of my outsized body in it, which I do quite regularly on winter evenings, once the fire is going. When we had our Depression-era bungalow remodelled, we had a consultation with the contractor, and my wife said she wanted a bay window next to the bathtub. The contractor dismissed the idea, saying "That just isn't done." In retrospect I did feel a bit sorry for the contractor, who said precisely the wrong thing to my wife. So now from the perspective of the tub I can look out through our lovely bay window onto a yew hedge, a hawthorn tree and several hectares of night sky.

The living room woodstove only suggests hedonistic enjoyment, but the bathtub is explicit about it. I can lounge in its warmth and openly acknowledge my reverence for its creature comforts. Immersion in gloriously warm water is an incredible human privilege. If I were to claim a religious affiliation, it would have to be Bathatarian. I have established an in-bath sacramental genuflection that also serves as a stretching exercise. Sitting in the tub cross-legged, lotus-style, I face the taps and slowly, very slowly, bend forward until my forehead gently and reverentially touches the faucet. Every religion requires a yin/yang, heaven/hell duality: mine is faucet/drain. Sometimes I will take more than one bath a day. If I were to have a spirit name, it would be Takes Two Baths.

Occasionally, I read in the bath, which is risky; one false move can destroy a book. There is far less at stake with a newspaper, but its sheer size makes for awkward arm positions. I haven't yet taken to writing in the bath, aside from jotting the odd note to myself, but if I did, I would be following in the grand literary bathtub-writing traditions of Jean-Paul Marat, Benjamin Franklin, Dalton Trumbo and Agatha Christie. I gather bathtub writing is a fairly common practice since a variety of special trays is commercially available, upon which to place one's notebook and wine glass.

A long bath followed by a longer read in front of the fire is sublime. One of the joys of the woodstove is its total lack of electronic controls. The Peltier fans on top start up and shut down when they feel like it, so they don't count. In fact, the woodstove's only control is the single manual damper lever. There is nothing to wear out, other than the stove's braided fibreglass door gasket, which gets replaced every few years. Once a year, the chimney sweep technician comes by. We always get a positive report card because we make each evening's fire end with a hot bang and not a cool, creosote-producing whimper. That is the least we can do for this steady and lifelong friend.

17
TURTLE NAIVETE

TURTLES AND TORTOISES are profoundly rooted in the human psyche. They have held great symbolic and mythic power across many cultures and times. The world is actually the carapace of a turtle, and we humans arose from the dirt in between the forty-five separate scutes. This origin story is from the First Nations of Eastern Canada, but variations of it are found in other cultures around the world. The Turtle Island allegory makes explicit our responsibility to care for this complex and timeless reptile that inhabits both land and water. In the language of biologists, the turtle is an umbrella species; look after it, and many other species will benefit.

Hindu mythology has the world supported by four elephants standing on the back of a turtle. This raises the question about what the turtle is standing on, which apparently is another turtle, and so on, making this creature the mascot of the epistemological concept of infinite regression.

Folk tales and fables have often featured turtles outsmarting their faster, stronger animal rivals. As our pre-scientific ancestors observed these slow-moving, long-lived, ever watchful and rather mysterious creatures, it is logical they would credit them with an intelligence that put them above the normal animal fray.

Children's books abound with turtle characters. One of my grandsons, who is now six, is totally bonded to turtles. He sleeps with a turtle stuffy with the unlikely name of Guida, and he frequently charges around the house in his turtle costume, complete with hood, padded carapace and tail. I too have a childhood connection: as a kid in California, I had a common box tortoise, who stumped contentedly around the backyard, munching on the shrubbery. His poops looked very much like small, fat cigars. Along with turtles, I was also heavily invested in snakes and lizards. As a thirteen-year old I kept a detailed "Reptile Record" in which I posted entries like this one:

> March 2, 1959. Alligator lizard (Gerrhontus) caught under boards in gully. Largest to date at 14 inches.

At about the same time, I was fascinated by Holling Clancy Holling's young-adult book *Paddle-to-the-Sea* (1941), his lavishly illustrated story of a carved toy canoe that makes its way from Lake Superior all the way to the Atlantic Ocean, encountering all manner of animals and adventures along the way. Later I discovered Holling's *Minn of the Mississippi* (1951), a large-format book that combines the life history of a snapping turtle with the account of its epic and fictitious journey from the headwaters of the Mississippi River to the Gulf of Mexico. Rereading this book now, I am still transported by Holling's incredibly detailed and colourful full-page paintings, and by his small black-and-white illustrations along the book's margins, which amplified the story with details of snapping turtle biology. Equally striking is Holling's blatant stereotyping of the Indigenous characters in his narratives, probably quite unexceptional at the time but very jarring now.

Distinguishing between land turtles, sea turtles and tortoises, it turns out, is just taxonomic hairsplitting. Tortoises are actually in the turtle group (Testudinidae), but they just happen to have stumpy feet and stay on land. Sea turtle feet are elongated into flippers, and land turtle feet are somewhere in between, giving them mobility on both land and water. Hurray for the taxonomy geeks who recognized that all three creatures are essentially the same: equally ancient, and equally mysterious. Somehow, all three of these creatures project an air of world-wise, and world-weary, detachment.

Many decades after my childhood box tortoise experience, I renewed my connection, this time with the western painted turtle

(*Chrysemys picta*). This species has a vast and curious distribution, starting from southern BC and spreading eastward all the way across southern Canada to the Atlantic Coast, then southward down into the US Gulf States, and then back up through the American Midwest. The species has been divided into a number of subspecies, including the BC coastal and the BC intermountain populations, which are slightly different. Both populations are considered species at risk. Western painted is the northernmost, and only, land turtle native to BC, found in ponds as far north as the fifty-first parallel. In rough terms, that parallel passes through Clinton, Revelstoke and Golden.

The greatest loss of BC painted turtle habitat has been in the Okanagan Valley, mostly due to pond drainage and river channellization. A few years ago, the Okanagan Basin Water Board asked me to look into what we could do to enhance the remaining pond habitat for turtles, and we settled on a small project to install basking logs. We had noticed that existing logs were often quite crowded and dominated by the larger adults, sometimes stacked two or three deep. We felt additional logs for the teenagers might be a nice gesture.

In preparation for the project, I did some background reading. Naively, I thought turtles simply liked to expose their naked flesh to the sunshine, rather like German tourists. It turns out turtle basking is actually a metabolic requirement. Western painteds do their omnivorous feeding underwater, generally near the pond's bottom, where temperatures are much lower than ambient. As cold-blooded species, turtles must warm up again for several hours in order to complete their digestion. If they can't bask, they starve.

In another case of abysmal Testudinal ignorance, I thought turtles would much prefer their basking logs to be situated in the middle of a pond, rather than attached to the shoreline, since they would be safe from land-based predators. Wrong again. My test case was Munson Pond, a lovely ten-hectare waterbody in southeast Kelowna, where we installed a basking raft in the middle of the pond, and a basking log anchored to the shore but floating in the water. A week after the installation, I came back to inspect. The log was completely colonized by turtles, and the raft by ducks.

The big cottonwood trees surrounding Munson Pond all have their trunks carefully wrapped with wire mesh, so inconvenient urban beavers don't cut them down. This of course eliminates a major source of turtle basking logs. The mesh is purely for the benefit of us human tourists that stroll the pathway around the pond. The cottonwoods really don't care; they adjusted to beaver harvesting several millennia ago. In response to the mesh fencing, the beavers have shifted their attention to the smaller unfenced cottonwoods, which are too small to qualify as basking logs. As a consequence, the turtles have to queue up to get on the few that remain. Urban nature does try its best to carry on.

Like sea turtles, western painteds lay their eggs on land, travelling as much as half a kilometre from their home pond to find appropriate soft, sandy ground in order to excavate a hole, deposit their eggs and then bury them. They will also move from one pond to another in search of food, mates or new habitat. This navigating ability has intrigued the animal behaviourists, who have performed all manner of studies with turtles, putting them in unfamiliar habitats to see how they find their way. The results were largely inconclusive, but did prove the point that "challenging environments tend to produce animals with advanced cognitive abilities." Too bad that hasn't worked for me.

The environment for a western painted turtle in the Okanagan is about as challenging as it gets, with pond drainage, fertilizer-induced pond eutrophication, climate change, road mortality, shortage of basking logs, plowed-up nesting habitat, Norway rats predating the eggs, and so on. And yet, these turtles persist. No wonder they seem world-weary.

Turtles are remarkably long-lived and tortoises even more so, putting elephants to shame. The English naturalist Gilbert White acquired a mature North African tortoise from his aunt in 1780:

> The old Sussex tortoise, that I have mentioned to you so often, is become my property. I dug it out of its winter

dormitory in March last, when it was enough awakened to express its resentments by hissing; and, packing it in a box with earth, carried it eighty miles in post-chaises....as it will now be under my eye, I shall now have an opportunity of enlarging my observations on its mode of life, and propensities.

White kept the tortoise, named Timothy, until the naturalist died many years later, followed shortly by his tortoise. Timothy was posthumously determined to be many decades old, and female. Her carapace is now in the British Museum. The longest documented tortoise lifespan is that of Harriet, who died in an Australian zoo at the ripe old age of 175. But there is speculation among turtle circles (the Testudinati) that they can actually live much longer than that, possibly four hundred or five hundred years.

My visits to Okanagan ponds gave birth to a compulsive desire to swim with turtles. Certainly, this was a tamer goal than swimming with dolphins or running with bulls, and would have the additional benefit of giving me first-hand experience of turtle habitat. For my maiden attempt, I hiked in to a fairly remote pond in the Marron Valley that I knew had plenty of turtles. Stripping down, I donned my mask and snorkel, and very quietly stepped into the water. In spite of size 14 feet, I sank immediately up to my knees in warm, clingy mud. My legs were immobilized. This was a dilemma. If I went down on hands and knees, I would then be completely immobilized. Somehow, I had to get out deep enough that buoyancy would keep me from sinking so far into the mud, and then lie down into the water and start swimming. Lifting a leg up meant I had to overcome the amazing suction force of this very clingy Marron Valley mud. After a series of herculean leg lifts, I finally got to chest-deep water, adjusted my swim mask, lay down, freed my feet for the last time, and became water-borne.

I have always revelled in that first moment of immersion, whether it be in ocean, river, lake, swimming pool and now a turtle pond. The bracing cold, the tingling of the entire skin, the sense of being a temporary visitor in an alien yet welcoming environment: all these

The Sky and the Patio

sensations come together in a sensual aquatic headrush. So there I was finally, my dream realized, paddling slowly through rich turtle water, but my visibility was absolutely nil. I was immersed in a spectacular algae bloom. I could not even see my hands.

After that experience, I tried another pond that had clearer water. The turtles of that pond probably saw this enormous, pale organism invading their habitat, and immediately dove for deep cover. So the dream of swimming with turtles is still on my bucket list. Another item on the list is to enter the shallows of Okanagan Lake equipped with snorkel, mask, fins and spear gun, to kill an invasive and destructive common carp.

The Marron Valley turtle pond experience raised another, less frivolous topic, that of connectivity. The pond is adjacent to a country road, and a brand new reptile and amphibian underpass had been installed. It was a large metal culvert with a flat bottom that passed under the road, and solid wing fences on either side to funnel creatures into the culvert instead of over the road. This project was a belated recognition of two fundamental facts in the lives of turtles, snakes, lizards, frogs, toads and salamanders: first, they don't stay in one place, and second, the impacts of road mortality on their populations are enormous.

I was quite intrigued by the construction of this new underpass. Bending down to look into it, I noticed a rectangular metal box firmly secured to the top of the culvert. Mystified, I looked more closely, and saw a small hole in the centre of the box. As I gawked, the slow realization dawned: this was a motion-activated camera, designed to record usage of the underpass. I subsequently found out the camera was part of a research project of Thompson Rivers University in Kamloops. So I envision the following, somewhat disturbing scenario:

TRU grad student downloads a summer's worth of underpass camera data onto her computer. She sits at her desk and methodically scrolls through the captured images: Western painted turtle, Check. Long-toed salamander, Check. Gopher snake, Check. Enormous bearded face with quizzical look...! It must have been a rude shock.

Ecological connectivity covers a range of scales, from a turtle going three hundred metres from pond to nest, to a wide-ranging wolf or grizzly going three hundred kilometres, to migrating birds or fish travelling three thousand kilometres. Connectivity writ large embraces water to land, valley bottom to alpine, forest to grassland, south to north, west to east, steep terrain to moderate and dozens of other habitat-to-habitat connections, including the reciprocal of each. Connectivity is now profoundly important, as climate change forces species to keep up with their rapidly shifting habitats and ecosystems. Caring for an individual species is a tangible act, caring for habitat is somewhat less so, and caring for connectivity is a very new and rather abstract notion. Starting with the small-scale, obvious linkages, like the underpass between turtle pond and turtle nest, is the first step toward a collective understanding of the broad scope of ecological connectivity.

As Minn, the snapping turtle, proceeds on her journey down the Mississippi River, author Holling has her displaying human emotions — fear, joy, anticipation and so on. Anthropomorphizing animals has a long tradition in literature, all the way from Aesop to Winnie the Pooh. It is a device now mostly confined to children's books. As an adult rereading the book, I cringe a bit when Minn recognizes the shadow of a boat above her, or is happy when she finds a safe pond, but I acknowledge the bonding power of anthropomorphism in children's books. Why else would someone grow up to actually care about turtles, let alone give them a second thought? Now, if we can just figure out a way to anthropomorphize the atmosphere.

Travelling Highway 97 on occasional trips to Kelowna, I pass a little pond sandwiched between the Coquihalla Connector and Gorman's sawmill. Someone has anchored a basking log in the pond. On my summer trips, I slow down slightly as I approach and take a quick, calculated glance at the basking log. If there is a western painted turtle on it, I know everything is right with the world.

18
THE NATURAL HISTORY OF THE BOOKSHELF

OUR SMALL LIVING room has a will of its own, as it strives for a kind of Victorian identity. Woodstove, pressed-tin wood box, oak hutch, glass-fronted bookshelf and curtains of heavy red velvet all speak of a shabby 1890s gentility. A stained-glass lampshade and framed reproductions of Albert Bierstadt and Albrecht Dürer add to the impression. My wife and I never consciously chose this motif; rather, it simply developed over the years as we were both drawn to the same items in second-hand stores and garage sales. Married couples often clash over interior décor, but we seem to have identical oak-infused, brass-knobbed and paisley-influenced tastes. Perhaps there is some genetic basis.

The glass-fronted bookshelf is a battered wooden relic, probably from the era just after the Victorian, when office furniture still retained a shred of elegance and the manual typewriter was dominant. Each of the four shelves has a framed window in front, which can be lifted and slid back to expose the books inside. The bottom part of the bookshelf consists of a series of shallow wooden pull-out drawers for letterhead stationery, forms and so on. Each drawer has a finger-sized hole at the bottom to facilitate paper removal.

I acquired the bookshelf years ago when the government office I worked in was being closed down. The outmoded and unused item was in need of minor repair and had been tagged for "offsite storage." I knew exactly what that phrase meant, so I removed the bookshelf covertly, as a pre-retirement gift. The repairs were straightforward,

The Sky and the Patio

and it now sits in our living room next to a comfortable overstuffed armchair, containing favourite books, plus a few that might be considered antiquarian. A few of the volumes are from my father, favourites when he was young, that he passed on to me. One such is Will James's *Smoky the Cowhorse*, from 1929. And there are three Tarzan novels, published 1912–1914. Tipped into one of the novels is a note from the author Edgar Rice Burroughs himself, obviously in response to a childhood note my father wrote. It says, "I have a dog too, and he gives me great pleasure."

The rest of the living room's bookshelves are standard open-fronted ones, containing an engagingly random assortment. There is a series of Russian novels, heavily weighted toward Maxim Gorky and Dostoevsky, from my high-school Bolshevik days. A section on Sacco and Vanzetti abuts publications about the Great Spokane Flood, which are next to the entire Dr. Seuss oeuvre. Not far from those are novels of the magic realists Gabriel García Márquez and Mario Vargas Llosa, and the poems and stories and essays of Jorge Luis Borges. Then there is the four-volume boxed set of the *Calvin and Hobbes* comic strip. And so forth.

I decided to organize my books. The origin of this impulse is obscure, but since I started acquiring books some fifty years ago, this seemed like a decent interval. And a fitting activity for the depths of winter when the days are short and the woodstove burns long. I own more than a hundred titles, but probably less than five hundred. Somehow, it seemed crass to actually count them.

To actually begin ordering this book collection, I first needed some kind of organizing principle. Alphabetical would be pedantic, and silly for such a small library. Dewey Decimal? Too impersonal. Fiction/nonfiction made some sense, but how would I accommodate the Annie Dillards, the Wallace Stegners or the James Agees, who wrote elegantly in both genres? A friend suggested if I couldn't come up with anything else, I should do it by jacket colour. Another idea, gleaned from an interior design magazine: turn all the books around, spine in, so as to achieve "a consistent aesthetic against white walls." Seriously?

The Natural History of the Bookshelf

Assuming I could get all the books newly ordered into rational categories, then I would have to decide which categories go on which bookshelf. Recently, I installed a new floor-to-ceiling shelf in the living room, and right away realized that vertical book positioning plays a major visual role. The upper contents of this tall bookshelf are at eye level, so I look at them often, whereas the lower bookshelves don't get the same level of visual attention. Ask any bookstore person: the books that get seen are the ones that get purchased. Books at eye level get all the love: books at ankle level are pretty much orphans. To make matters even worse, we have some overflow books on shelves in an upstairs guest bedroom. This is a boon to literary house guests, but for me these books only assert themselves on my infrequent trips upstairs.

Any search for an organizing principle first requires a review of what is to be organized, so I began going title by title, bookshelf by bookshelf, with many interesting stops along the way. The mathematics of bicycle gearing. Jane Jacobs's revolutionary principles of urban planning. Early painters of the Canadian Rockies. As I made my way along the titles, I began to realize that many of my current interests and preoccupations actually germinated years or even decades ago, as evidenced by the old book purchases. Aging along with ones' books is not only a sensual pleasure, but also an opportunity for self-rediscovery. The personal library as a tangible record of the fascinations that have endured, as well as some few that have not.

Some books, as Borges has pointed out, sit quietly on your bookshelf, reading themselves. Having already read them, you know their memorable parts, and a mere glance at the cover is enough to bring those passages to mind. Such is the case with the books of New Age anthropologist William Irwin Thompson; a passage in one of them, read some twenty years ago, still somehow resonated. Unfortunately, I did not remember the passage itself, only the fact that it was memorable. So I reread his entire 1981 book *The Time Falling Bodies Take to Light* (I am still in awe of that title), without finding the passage. Digging further, I rediscovered it in another book of his, *At the Edge of History* (1971):

> We will have to come right up to the edge to find out where we are, and who we are. At the edge of history, history itself can no longer help us, and only myth remains equal to reality. What we know is less than what we are, and so the politics of miracle must be unacceptable to our knowledge to be worthy of our being. Credo quia absurdum est. The future is beyond knowing, but the present is beyond belief. We make so much noise with technology that we cannot discover that the stargate is in our foreheads. But the time has come; the revelation has already occurred, and the guardian seers have seen the lightning strike the darkness we call reality. And now we sleep in the brief interval between the lighting and the thunder.

Thompson was obviously confident of an impending tectonic shift in human consciousness. He passed on in 2020, but I am guessing he was sorely disappointed in what he saw of the twenty-first century.

I had to look up the Latin phrase Thompson used: it means "I believe it because it is absurd."

My office was not to be part of the reorganization, but it got swept up in this new and unexpected self-rediscovery anyway. The office's semi-chaotic mass of scientific journal reprints, pamphlets and books was daunting. Why did I collect all those papers on elk-cattle conflicts? Or the ones on the wetlands of the Okanagan? Or on the philosophy of science? Not to mention the stacks of literature on fire ecology. One of the papers I stumbled upon was "Detection of Large Woody Debris Accumulation in Old-Growth Forests Using Sonic Wave Collection." This is a delightful send-up of scientific journal writing, penned by Indiana R. Jones and Ethan Allen ("Et Al" for short), of the Department of Philosophical Biology of Earl's Corner Bar in Hoople, North Dakota. Jones and Allen attempt to determine whether a falling tree in the Chequamegon National Forest makes a sound if no one is there to hear it. Results were inconclusive, but the authors did prove a very solid inverse correlation between alcohol consumption and the ability to correctly pronounce "Chequamegon."

Every person who writes either burns their early efforts in disgust or else hoards them obsessively. I am on the obsessive side, but more passive-obsessive: my instincts are less about hoarding and more about a general unwillingness to throw things away (which, now that I say it, sounds a bit redundant). But as part of the bookshelf process, I did review boxes and files of old writing, and that definitely put me into the big leagues of New Age self-discovery. Mostly, what I learned about myself was how arrogant I was as a young man, plus how easy it was to get poorly written drivel published back in the early glory days of CanLit, and how hard it is now. But I did find reference to a few passions that began in my teens and, like fire in the woodstove, lay as quiescent but enduring embers that would flare up randomly over subsequent decades.

The organizational review process, which morphed into a haphazard journey of self-discovery, was essentially a search for change — or lack of change — over time. Scientists would refer to these as longitudinal studies. Much of my ecological work has also been devoted to documenting changes over time, by monitoring grazing exclosures, studying fire scars, reading early explorers' journals and studying archival landscape photos. Perhaps the true motive behind my longitudinal studies is a romantic desire for a return to a pre-European contact, Arcadian landscape. But in more pragmatic terms, longitudinal studies are tremendously useful for predicting the near future. How accurate would our climate change predictions be, for instance, if scientists had not started tracking levels of atmospheric carbon dioxide in the 1950s?

In the end, the longitudinal study of myself — using books as a surrogate — was interesting but inconclusive. Way too many variables.

The Sky and the Patio

One of our living room bookshelves is devoted to what I would call, quaintly, natural history. *Grass Systematics, The Mosses of British Columbia, Okanagan Geology,* and so forth. Stacks of literature on the ecology of this Okanagan of mine, not surprising given this valley's importance as Canada's biodiversity hotspot.

But even here, within the natural history section, clear organizational boundaries are difficult. Where to put Loren Eiseley or Barry Lopez, for instance? And Jorge Luis Borges, who fiercely occupied the entire range of literature? Here he is defending his right to add a star to the firmament, as an allegory for the human imagination:

> With the ambitious gesture of a man who, contemplating the astral generosity of the spring sky, would crave yet another star and, dark in the bright night, would demand that constellations shatter their incorruptible destiny and renew their flame with signs unseen by the ancient gaze of sailors and shepherds, I sounded my throat once, imploring the incontrovertible heaven of art to sanction our gift for appending unforeseen lights and braiding into stunning crowns the perennial stars.

Borges's statement of his poetic rights ranks right up there with Walt Whitman's:

> I sound my barbaric yawp over the roofs of the world.

Our bedroom bookshelf is the repository for whatever I have brought in with me for bedtime reading, plus a few other volumes I have consciously placed there. The theory behind the conscious placements runs like this: "I've been meaning to read this one for months and if I put it here by my bed I might get desperate enough to pick it up." The bedroom shelf also contains a few hefty books that I don't read cover to cover, but that I enjoy opening randomly, like Simon Schama's *Landscape and Memory*, or *A Pattern Language*, by Christopher Alexander.

Then there is the apocrypha shelf, containing books I don't know what to do with. Like an aquarium book, but I gave the aquarium away long ago. A flora of a region I'd once hoped to visit, but now likely never will. A self-help book — not a chance I'll ever read it. All of these are candidates for our local thrift shop, where they might find a new home and be loved.

Speaking of the thrift shop, I have a friend who has the largest personal collection of books I've ever seen. A retired antiquarian bookseller, he is getting up in years and has put his collection up for sale. Sadly, no one wants to buy it, a sign of these digital times. But I often meet him coming out of the thrift shop, with books under his arm.

If I were ever to write a treatise called *Great Used Bookstores I Have Known*, Main Street Books in Penticton would figure prominently. Floor-to-ceiling shelves, narrow aisles, carpeted floor, classical music playing quietly in the background. The men and women staffing the place move about quietly, devoted adherents to a profound theocracy of books. The more obscure your request, the greater the pleasure they take in seeking it out for you. Once you're in the store and your request has been located, it is easy to slip into a timeless state and drift slowly down the aisles. This is browsing at its most ethereal level. The store's volumes are organized, but not to excess. The staff recognize the value of serendipity.

An intriguing aspect of my library reorganization process was the discovery of various frontispiece inscriptions from authors, and my own faint pencil underlines and book darts or torn bits of paper marking particular pages. Another longitudinal opportunity we lose as we shift to digital is the ability to see if that marked book passage that resonated for us five or thirty years ago still resonates, or not.

As reading becomes more and more digital, I think we will miss the tactile pleasure of actually holding a book, plus missing all those inscriptions, marked pages and underlined passages that were important to us at the time. For instance, my father's copy of *Smoky the Cowhorse* bears the inscription "Merry Christmas

The Sky and the Patio

from your loving aunt, December 1929." That inscription places me directly into the time and mindset of my father at age twelve, dreaming of riding through western sage on a saddle bronc.

Perhaps I'm just a Luddite. My trepidations about the e-book are probably identical to the concerns of ancient keepers of parchment scrolls as they fearfully contemplated the advent of book printing.

Something calls me away from my library organizing effort. It is evening, when red velvet curtains, a woodstove, an overstuffed chair and random books on the oak coffee table beckon. In the end, this project came down to a bit of dusting, straightening and reading, and some very limited reshuffling. My vague organizing principle was simply no match for the fierce independence of these wonderful books.

19
THE PANTHEON OF DUSTY HEROES

THEY RIDE BY, these heroes in my pantheon, each in period costume. In focus for a brief moment, they stay just beyond my grasp and then disappear again, into the fog of history. Ranald MacDonald is one of those. I can never quite catch him, to pin him down into literary form. How do I commit this man, one of the first Europeans to penetrate closed Japan, this seafarer, gold miner, explorer, teacher and BC cattle rancher, to paper? Do I render his complex and multiple lives into biography, novel, epic poem or history?

Here are the bare bones. Ranald is born in 1824 at Fort Astoria, on the remote Oregon coast. He is the son of a Hudson's Bay Company factor, Archibald MacDonald. His mother, Koale'xoa, is Chinook royalty, but she dies shortly after Ranald's birth. Growing up in the company fort, Ranald befriends a couple of young Japanese fishermen whose vessel had blown adrift in a Pacific storm, and who were living out their lives as Oregon castaways. They converse by means of the utilitarian second language of that time and place: Chinook. As an adolescent, Ranald is sent overland to attend the Red River Academy. As he grows to manhood, Ranald conceives a mysterious and compelling connection between Japan and his mother's people. Graduating from the academy, he works briefly as a bank clerk in St. Thomas, Ontario. Tiring of colonial life, where his Metis status puts him on the outside looking in, he heads south and finds work on a steamboat heading down the Mississippi River. Reaching New Orleans, he ships aboard a whaling vessel headed to the Sea of Japan. Upon reaching the whaling grounds, MacDonald pays the skipper to cast him adrift in an oarless lifeboat near Rishiri, a tiny volcanic island off the tip of northern Japan. This is in 1848, and MacDonald knows the mortal risks; he puts himself at the mercy of a country totally closed to foreigners, years before Commodore Perry's famous visit.

What ensues is a fruitful year in Japan, first with the indigenous Ainu on Rishiri, and then in Nagasaki under token house arrest. He learns Japanese and teaches English; several of his students go on to be translators as Japan later opens its doors to the rest of the world.

Leaving Japan in 1849, MacDonald heads to Australia for a gold rush, and then proceeds to Scotland. Home finally beckons, and he arrives just in time for BC's Cariboo gold rush. For a time, he mucks for gold in Horsefly, but soon discovers a better lifestyle as a packer, bringing food and supplies to hungry miners. Next, he runs a toll ferry across the Fraser River at Lillooet. From there, he moves on to Cache Creek, to operate a cattle ranch. Ever mindful of the Orient, he explores the possibilities of an overland route from the Cariboo to tidewater at Bella Coola. And he works as a packer on Robert Brown's 1864 Vancouver Island Exploring Expedition.

Sometimes I go out for coffee, and then take a walk in the park.

Ranald never marries, but he has lots of kin, folks that are important to him later in life. He helps a cousin run a provisioning depot in Kamloops; Christina Lake is named after another cousin. He eventually settles near Fort Colville, where he becomes the subject of a notorious published interview by General George Custer's widow.

Ranald lives out his old age in the Colville area, trying unsuccessfully to get his memoirs about Japan published. In 1894, while visiting a relative, he falls ill. A few months later, he dies quietly at age 70, taking his secrets with him.

Years ago, I tracked down Ranald MacDonald's grave. It sits by itself near Toroda, a tiny Washington community just across the line from Midway, BC. The gravesite is adjacent to the meandering

The Pantheon of Dusty Heroes

Kettle River, in a little bunchgrass prairie surrounded by ponderosa pine. Embedded at the foot of the gravestone are two rocks from Rishiri Island. The gravestone lists his parents and the countries he visited. Below that are two words: Sayonara, Farewell.

I took a picture of myself standing next to the gravestone, hoping to capture some of the elusive spirit and motives of this man. So far, it hasn't worked, and I still have no idea of how to commit him to paper. Maybe in a movie script. In the meantime, Ranald MacDonald makes occasional appearances in my pantheon. I see him come into focus momentarily, on horseback. Wearing a dusty frock coat, he looks to the far horizon. What momentous, globe-spanning landscapes those dark eyes have seen. Passing by, he looks back and gives me a knowing, conspiratorial wink. And then he is gone, leaving the rest up to me.

20
CLIMATE CHANGE

I AM A full participant in our hell-bent, petroleum-based economy, being the owner of a twenty-year old Ford Explorer. The Explorer's back bumper has a faded sticker that says STOP THE TRANS MOUNTAIN PIPELINE, relic of a battle long since lost. One day, I parked the Ford on the street by our post office. As I got out, a red-haired guy in a big, black, late-model F-350 pickup with dulies pulled up alongside and rolled down his window. "So is your Ford an electric vehicle?" he asks.

I was caught unawares, and said, "Nah, it's old-school."

He shook his head, and in an angry voice replied, "Then how the hell are you going to get gas for it if you shut down Trans Mountain?"

My jaw dropped. I began formulating a lengthy response about the true costs of the pipeline: crude oil exports to the world's biggest carbon emitter, China; endangered orca habitats; full-cost tar sands carbon accounting, toxic diluents, mass transit, bicycle lanes, personal carbon footprints. But before I could say anything, the red-haired guy rolled up his window, gunned his enormous pickup's engine, and sped off.

This was a brief but very significant encounter, one that got me thinking. In truth, the red-haired guy and I are very much alike. Neither one of us is shy about voicing our opinions. We've both been duped into thinking that gas-guzzling pickup trucks are proof of masculinity; in fact, testosterone seems to be a very effective chemical precursor to carbon dioxide. I do resent the hordes of oversized pickup trucks, many with Alberta plates, that

The Sky and the Patio

commute on our main valley thoroughfare, Highway 97, with no passengers and no payload. Mr. Redhair loves the petroleum-based economy, and probably commutes to an oil-sands job up in northern Alberta. I, for my part, hate the petroleum-based economy, and drive my old Ford as little as possible. The harsh reality remains, however: both the red-haired guy and I are full participants in the carbon-based economy, and neither of us is smarter than the boiling frog.

My only defence, my refuge, is irony. I drive my Explorer infrequently, I burn wood in our stove, and on rare occasions I get on an airplane. My reusable shopping bag is made from cloth, but even as a woke grocery shopper, I am plagued with assorted single-use plastic food wrappers and trays. Unlike Mr. Redhead, I am sinfully aware of the impacts of my own and Canada's carbon footprint — and how little we are doing to reduce it. But somehow it gives me comfort to sardonically revel in that knowledge.

Irony is a curious thing: instantly recognizable, but hard to define. The ancient Greeks called it "simulated ignorance." We use irony all the time, almost unconsciously. When something doesn't go as expected, we say "Oh, great," or "Nice." There is a variant called dramatic irony, where the audience knows some crucial piece of information that the character onstage is blissfully unaware of. Irony in all its forms is delightful; it adds interesting dimensions to normal banter, makes us feel clever, and lets us appear to be in control of a situation when we aren't. Irony is a comfortable hiding place.

My first delicious taste of carbon irony came in that same hulking Ford automobile of mine, back when climate change was first emerging as a public topic, and the denier debate was in full swing. I was on my way from the Okanagan to Vancouver to attend a conference on climate change. Halfway there, somewhere outside of Princeton, I suddenly realized a monumental and very personal irony: here I was, alone, driving an enormous Ford Explorer gas pig to a climate change conference.

Needless to say, there is a fundamental link between fossil carbon and internal combustion. As the brilliant writer and energy critic Andrew Nikiforuk points out, the world's very first internal combustion engines were steam-driven pumps, used to drain water out of coal mines.

Delving further into our individual responses to climate change (here abbreviated as CC), I have developed several categories:

FLAGRANT DENIER
Denies human-caused CC; supports fracking, pipelines and big pickups; leaves the engine idling even in midsummer.

DENIER
Denies human-caused CC; maintains usual lifestyle.

TECHNOPOSITIVE
Accepts CC; maintains usual lifestyle, confident we can solve CC with new technology.

MEH
Accepts that CC is happening, and that it will destroy the planet. What's for lunch?

FATALIST
Accepts CC; maintains usual lifestyle, knowing we are unwilling or unable to stop CC.

OSTRICH
Accepts it but is too passive or too overwhelmed to change lifestyle.

PASSIVE TOKENIST (most of us)
Accepts it; makes token changes to lifestyle; donates $50/year to environmental organizations.

PASSIVE IRONIC (put me here)
Understands the magnitude and threat of CC; makes

token changes to lifestyle; revels in personal and political apathy in the face of an existential threat.

ACTIVIST
Understands CC; makes major lifestyle changes; becomes a climate activist.

OFF-GRID
Understands CC; goes off-grid; reduces C footprint to near zero.

OLD TESTAMENT
Accepts CC; rejoices at the arrival of the End Times.

Another irony I live with on a daily basis is the aforementioned plastic food packaging. It is truly remarkable how deeply plastics have become embedded in our food system, and now, with the advent of microplastics, in our bloodstream as well. I know our town's landfill will recycle some of the plastics if I took them there, but where to store the damn things until I'm ready to make a landfill run? Mounting kitchen frustration finally led to a solution. As I wait patiently for Canada to ban all single-use plastic food wrapping, I store mine temporarily in our rarely used dishwasher. Easy access, convenient, and if we need to do a load of dishes after a big dinner party, it is easy enough to remove the bags temporarily. So now every two months or so I empty the dishwasher and take the bags to Summerland's landfill, and do my best to sort them into their appropriate bins of "regular plastic," "crinkly plastic," "other plastic," "rigid Styrofoam" and "flexible Styrofoam." As kitchen climate change activist Anne-Marie Bonneau says, "We don't need a handful of people doing zero waste perfectly...we need millions of people doing it imperfectly."

Like most consumers, I don't know my polyethylene terephthalate from my polyvinyl chloride. Occasionally, I look on the underside of the plastic container and see the comforting triangle made of arrows, with a number, 1, 2, 3, 4, 5, 6 or 7, inside. I am told that plastics 1, 2 and 3 are recyclable, the rest not so much. The truth is almost all of it goes to a landfill, somewhere. And into the ocean, and our bloodstreams.

One of the comfortably false notions that we Technopositives and Passive Ironists take comfort in is the belief that we can simply wait until industry delivers efficient, affordable, mass-produced electric vehicles. Then we can retire our Ford Explorers and big black trucks, switch to electric vehicles and continue our current lifestyle, with nary a blip. Right. Irony, again.

I recently had what I am calling my Bartley Road Revelation, on a recent trip via Highway 97. The stoplight had turned red at this suburban Westbank intersection. I happened to be the first in my lane, so I had a panoramic view of four lanes of stopped through traffic, two lanes of left-turn traffic and two lanes of Bartley Road through traffic. A true multitude of vehicles, many of them big pickups, all pulsing eagerly in anticipation of the traffic light change. Behind each of the lead cars I could see the lengthy linear packs, each stretching hundreds of metres back from the intersection, all paused, all intent on the race to the next stoplight. At that moment, just before the light turned green, I had a blazing and profound insight: this is never going to stop. We are permanently addicted to the private automobile and the massive infrastructure it brings in its filthy wake. Perhaps this is another outcome of our settler mentality: seeing the land as a disposable surface to pave over and drive on.

Travelling up and down my Okanagan Valley makes me grind my teeth. At the same time as I navigate the overwhelming highway traffic, I see the suburban housing sprawl moving up the valley sides: two phenomena that feed on each other. Add in the oblivious frontier mentality, a gonzo real estate market, obsessive desires for lake-view homes, development-compliant local politicians and big-box shopping malls, and you have captured the human essence of the Okanagan. Fortunately, the rampant suburb developments are occasionally interrupted by stony, precipitous and unbuildable hillsides. We are a valley of gneiss and nail bars.

The Sky and the Patio

A transportation planner might look at a map of this valley and say, "Wow, what perfect geography for mass transit — roughly three hundred and fifty thousand people living in towns and cities all arranged in a 185-kilometre straight line, from Osoyoos to Salmon Arm! No loops, no feeder routes required! Not only that, but the main travel corridor, Highway 97, passes right through the centres of these towns and cities!" In reality, we are moving in the opposite direction, toward greater reliance on private automobiles and greater suburban sprawl. A recent billboard advertisement for an upscale suburban Kelowna housing development summed it up: "Close to nature, minutes from downtown." That is the destructive and ultimately unachievable Okanagan dream. The suburb extirpates nature and the commuter car kills the downtown.

Jane Jacobs, in her groundbreaking 1961 book *The Death and Life of Great American Cities*, argued persuasively for urban density, mixed use and pedestrian orientation. This was her formula for functional and culturally vibrant cities, towns and neighbourhoods. The Okanagan persists in going in the opposite direction, of car-dependent urban sprawl. Recently, I am seeing a trend toward downtown "super-density" consisting of high-rise apartment blocks, reminiscent of Soviet-style architecture. So we are sprawling at one extreme and super-densifying at the other, totally bypassing the Jacobs ideal of medium density and mixed use.

Our two valleys have the raw materials for a vibrant regional culture: climate, nature, agriculture, food, wine and talent. What we lack are inspiring conversations in coffee shops, literary conspiracies in brew pubs, artistic collaborations in wine bars and theatrical performances on Main Street. Those events are much more likely to happen when our downtowns evolve from mere collections of commerce and parking to actual, diverse, lived-in communities. Reducing urban sprawl and refocusing on intelligent urban densification would give us the fourfold benefit of enhancing local culture, protecting local ecosystems, minimizing community carbon footprint and reducing urban interface wildfire risk.

I have another feat of mental gymnastics, besides irony, that keeps me in my pathetic climate change comfort zone. At my age, some ways past three score and ten, my own death is no longer the abstraction it used to be. Climate change has allowed me to trade in fear of my own mortality for that of the planet. What a comfort, as long as I don't think about that grandson in his turtle costume.

The petroleum we suck out of the ground is there as the result of five previous global extinctions: what could possibly go wrong? Or as writer Kurt Vonnegut put it, what's wrong with "making thermodynamic whoopee with fossil fuels?"

Some thinkers say that petroleum was the midwife of capitalism, and that one cannot survive without the other. Others say the only way we can defeat climate change is to elect female politicians. I firmly believe that. There are very few examples of matriarchy in human history, and it shows. Viva la Matria.

My generation, that of the North American post-WWII baby boomers, is perhaps the most privileged, carefree and self-indulgent generation in the entire history of the planet. Not only that, I grew up in Southern California, the hallowed birthplace of this consumer generation. That was where car culture became dominant, where suburbs, freeways, drive-in fast-food restaurants and shopping malls were invented, and where, thanks to DuPont, we would all experience "better living through chemistry." My only pathetic and somewhat depressing defence: whenever I go to a climate change action meeting, baby boomers are typically in the majority.

I was chatting with a young friend in his early thirties, saying how the coming decades must appear particularly grim for him, since his generation will experience the full reality of climate change, whereas for my generation it has been mostly theoretical. He disagreed, saying "the coming decade will be very exciting, since it will bring us right up to the edge."

21
ALIENS, GOLF AND THE TROUT CREEK ECOLOGICAL RESERVE

WHEN I AM on the Trout Creek Ecological Reserve, a quiet hillside of bunchgrass and ponderosa pine, my nature reveries are often interrupted by two different shouts coming up from the back nine far down below. The shouts are both four-letter words, one of which is "Fore!"

British Columbia's ecological reserves originated with the International Biological Program of the 1960s. Similar to protected areas, ecological reserves were created to protect examples of BC's myriad of ecosystem types. These reserves prohibit motorized vehicles, bicycles, horses, cattle grazing and camping, but allow for educational visits and research work, which I have been doing on this Trout Creek Ecological Reserve (TCER) for two decades now.

Many of British Columbia's 154 reserves are tucked away in remote areas, but not this one. TCER is a ten-minute drive, plus a twenty-minute walk, from our house. Its lower portion lies hard by the Summerland Golf and Country Club's back nine. These two entities are disparate bedfellows, with no obvious similarities. The one tries for untouched wildness, allowing local native vegetation to set its own course, while the other imposes a uniquely human design: non-native species, intense management and abundant external inputs. One entity actively discourages human visitors, the other welcomes them with open arms. The sublime and the ridiculous. Yet these two Summerland examples seem to coexist, without any obvious friction.

The Sky and the Patio

The trail to TCER starts from the golf course, and I am keenly aware of the fundamental differences between the two as I drive into the course's crowded parking lot. Nattily dressed golfers are loading bags into carts, donning custom-fitted gloves and chatting with each other in anticipation of the first hole. In contrast — and not looking at all like a golfer — I attract mild curiosity as I don hiking boots and tuck my pantlegs into my socks to foil ticks. Then I load up my backpack with camera, GPS unit, granola, plant books, notebook, Daubenmire frame, pliers for removing cactus, and head off, cartless, on foot. My backpack probably has as many implements as a well-endowed golf bag.

TCER is small, only seventy-five hectares. Think fifty or so city blocks, bounded on the east, south and west by the surprisingly deep and precipitous Trout Creek Canyon, and on the north by an arbitrary boundary line. Nearly the whole reserve is south-facing, starting at 600 metres at the lip of the canyon, rising gently through a broad parkland of grass and ponderosas, then steeply through a mixed ponderosa/Douglas-fir forest, and finally topping out at 850 metres on a treeless rock knob covered with mosses and lichens. Level ground is a rarity here. Volcanoes, glaciers and forest fires have each had their way with this landscape over time. Given the vegetation, the elevation band and the geological history, this little pocket is a microcosm of the entire Okanagan Valley, from Osoyoos to Salmon Arm. In my dozens of visits to the reserve over the years, I have never encountered another person there. I'm not sure if I should be gratified or appalled by that.

Despite my many visits, there are still some gullies and knobs and swales I still don't know. As I explore, my visual focus tends to be right in front of my feet so I don't slip on loose rock or step on a cactus or a rattlesnake. The presence of the western diamondback rattler encourages what I call "active listening," particularly in summer, when they are out and about and the grass is tall. The rattling sound a dry balsamroot leaf makes if you brush past it can give you a start. But mature death camas, which keeps its loose seeds within dry pods, sounds just like a snake rattle. The "tell" is that the rattle stops as soon as you freeze, whereas a snake's rattle will continue on for a few seconds.

On my walks, I remind myself to stop and look up on occasion. Remembering specific landmarks can be problematic. "That veteran ponderosa next to the big rock," for instance, is useless, since there are so many examples. In this dry climate, the lee of a large rock is a favourable spot for a tree seedling to establish and survive.

Hearing the golfers in the distance reminds me of my first adolescent golf venture, when my father bought me a set of clubs. Prior to our first tee-off, Dad gave me a stern lecture about patience, composure and the importance of controlling my temper. By the third hole, my even-tempered father was cursing loudly, and at one point even flung his putter in rage after a close miss. That was my introduction to golf's hold on the male psyche.

As I got older, I came to associate golf with white male privilege, conservative politics and disdain for the environment. In spite of that, I surreptitiously enjoyed the game. I was careful not to play more than a few times a year, so in my own mind I could write the outings off as a lark, as merely seeing how the other half lives. Many decades after that inaugural round, I still play a few laughable games a year, stopping far short of letting my ego get involved. I still use those ancient clubs too: the Northwestern Shot Saver Marty Furgol Signature Series, circa 1962.

Years ago, one of my sons worked at a local golf course for a summer, and he showed me a copy of the course's annual order for chemical fertilizer, herbicides, fungicides and insecticides. The lengthy list literally made the hair stand up on the back of my neck.

I go to TCER for four reasons: exercise, science, education and nature reveries. Golfers share the exercise motive with me. For science they substitute rapt attention to putts, education for critiquing their companion's golf swing, and outdoor enjoyment for nature reveries. To each his own, I say.

The winding, barely visible trail from the golf course to TCER passes through lovely native fescue grassland. The twenty-minute walk it takes to reach it nicely provides for a mental decluttering and readjustment. Just short of the reserve, strategically positioned atop a low ridge, is a boulder, a glacial erratic the size of two refrigerators, lying on its side. I call it the Touching Rock. Its coarse granite surface hosts a lovely variety of lichens. Their muted greens and browns against the granite's speckled black and white create a wonderful pattern. I always stop at the Touching Rock and place my hand on its rough and sun-warmed surface for a time. From the rock's vantage point one can see a bit of Okanagan Lake to the east. Off to the south and across the canyon are the bizarre minarets of an erosional formation locally known as Crater Mountain, and to the southwest, the northern reaches of the Penticton Indian Reserve.

I have touched this rock on so many separate occasions that I now recognize my gesture has become a ritual. The great beauty of rituals is that they have none of the pervasive duality that our language imposes on us. A ritual just is; it transcends good/bad, past/present, us/them, human/nonhuman. As William Jordan says, ritual is a valuable tool in our social quest to re-establish connections with nature.

On one memorable visit to TCER, I accompanied Richard Armstrong, a respected elder from the Penticton Indian Band, together with a group of young people. Along the way, Richard would point out various birds and plants, giving the nsyilxcən name of each. One of the youngsters found the fragile half-shell of a bird egg and showed it to Richard, who told him the name of the bird species, both in English and nsyilxcən. A little farther on, the same young fellow picked up an errant golf ball. Holding it up to Richard, he asked in jest, "Mr. Armstrong, what bird is this from?" Richard replied, in all seriousness, "Well son, that is a condo egg."

Richard is right about the direct Okanagan connection between golf courses and condominiums; where you find one, you find the other. They are sympatric species. Fortunately, this golf course has none yet, but I can feel the ghosts of condos yet to come, hovering over its scenic lake-view hillsides.

Aliens, Golf and the Trout Creek Ecological Reserve

Our youth group continued their hike across TCER to the lip of the Trout Creek Canyon. The first view down into this precipitous canyon always triggers a moment of stunned silence, and this encounter was no different. Finally, one of the young people asked Richard about a strange landform on the other side. It was exactly half of a smooth inverted cone, with its broad base at the bottom of the canyon and its pointed tip at a level bench just across from where we stood. "Ah," said Richard, with his mischievous smile, "that's where the aliens landed."

Sometime later, I discovered Richard's aliens comment was not entirely in jest: the nsyilxcən place name for this area is "liq'sxn", which translates to "the place where a meteorite hit, a significant event where the people were scared and worried."

In the course of my fire history research on TCER, I discovered a contemporary companion to tree-ring and fire-scar analysis, in the form of repeat aerial photography. I was surprised to find good-quality aerial images of this area dating back to 1938, allowing me to document changes in tree cover by comparing those early airphotos with contemporary satellite photos. A BC government agency has digitized and preserved these old airphotos, along with the accompanying flight line maps. By studying these old maps, you can identify and order digital copies of specific photos. I am still trying to imagine the kind of airplane that would have been used in 1938.

While studying the old airphotos, I noticed some puzzling circular landforms near the present TCER. I worked through several possibilities, including crop circles, until it finally dawned: these were golf holes. Imagine, a golf course in a small, isolated Okanagan town in 1938! I spoke to a neighbour who works at the course; he informed me that the Summerland course, founded in 1925, is a relative youngster compared with the Vernon Golf and Country Club, which was founded in 1913. Digging further, I found that the Hedley Golf Course, on the banks of the Similkameen, was built in 1909! Golfers are nothing if not motivated. Perhaps there was some collective settler desire to transplant the golf and

The Sky and the Patio

country club tradition into the untamed wilds of the Okanagan, thus making British Columbia more British.

Comparing the old and new airphotos of TCER shows a dramatic increase in tree cover due to the suppression of fire, as discussed in an earlier chapter. The archetypal, pre-contact Okanagan Valley landscape was a parkland, with widely scattered veteran trees whose branch canopies started several metres above ground, together with a few juvenile and seedling trees scattered here and there. The contemporary landscape, in contrast, has legions of young trees, and many of the vets have canopies that reach right down to the ground.

An ecological reserve is a unique location to do vegetation monitoring, as it allows tracking of successional change in the absence of human disturbance. I have had the privilege of putting in a few permanent monitoring transects on TCER. One of the tests for success in this quixotic activity is the ability to relocate the transects you or some other researcher put in five or ten or twenty years ago. Because the sample size is typically embarrassingly small, say five twenty-five-metre-long transects representing an entire ecological site, accuracy is absolutely essential. You must find the points that mark the exact start and end of each transect, so you are monitoring the identical bits of ground that were originally monitored, thus substituting precision for replication. And monitoring needs to be done at roughly the same time of year, usually early summer, since some plants can vary considerably through the growing season.

Ten years seemed like a decent interval, and I had some Covid time on my hands, so I decided to redo my old Trout Creek transects. Because there are no vehicles, cows or bicycles allowed on ecological reserves, I was able to mark the original transects with straight rebar stakes protruding above ground. To make them more visible, I had slid sections of white PVC pipe down over each rebar. Easy-peasy: now just relocate the original stakes and do the monitoring. So again I proceeded through the golf course equipped with tape, Daubenmire frame, field notes and my memory of the six transects I had put in a decade ago. How hard could it be to find a mere twelve stakes on a landscape that I knew so well?

Several hours later, sweating and frustrated, I sat down on a rock outcrop to reassess. I had found two stakes, *not* representing a single transect pair, and had no idea where the rest were. The next day, I came back with my GPS unit and the UTM locations I had stored for the twelve points. After several hours, I found three more, but the GPS unit was giving me fits. Even the stakes I did find were not lined up precisely with their UTMs. Not enough satellites? Wobble in the earth's orbit? Russian interference?

There are many ways to lose a transect marking stake, including bad GPS data, but now I could add another one to my list: bears. Curious black bears had slid the white PVC pipes off several of the rebar pins, moved the pipes a distance, and proceeded to chew them, leaving obvious bite marks in the plastic. Fortunately, the bears found the plastic pipes inedible, and left them fairly close to their pins. My original plot map was beginning to make some sense, but I still had seven to go. The next day, I brought along the big gun: a metal detector. What a relief to finally relocate all the pins and begin the actual remonitoring. My neighbour golfers also have quests for lost objects. But they have an option I don't have: abandon the hunt, take a stroke, and play on with a new ball.

As I stretched my metre tape across the first transect, I felt a bit nervous; it had been a year or two since I had done any grassland monitoring, and I knew from my walks there were several plants that were familiar, but whose names now escaped me. So be it; I had a comprehensive plant list of TCER as a memory trigger, and if that failed, a dog-eared copy of *Plants of Southern Interior British Columbia* in my backpack.

Metre One. Slowly sliding the Daubenmire frame downward, its aperture instantly transformed into a one-tenth-metre window of beauty and analysis. I was back in the saddle.

In spite of fire suppression and the resulting forest encroachment, the grassland vegetation of TCER is in an advanced ecological stage. It is hard to put a single name to this condition, so I offer a few: climax, high seral, potential natural community. These multiple terms are a reflection of our ambiguity about ecological succession: Is it linear? Branching or circular? How far does it go? Is there an endpoint? Is there only one trajectory or many? How long is each stage? And do our theories need to be adjusted based on climate change? In the end, the understory vegetation of TCER can be described as relatively simple but highly evolved. It is composed of a couple of dominant bunchgrass species, plus a scattering of broadleaved plants and shrubs. Some invasives are present but they are not abundant, and a few rare plant species can be found. The conifer overstory is scattered ponderosa pine plus a few Douglas-fir. But this overall simplicity hides a great deal of history, resilience and stored carbon.

I am not the first to do science in TCER. In my usual literature deep dive, I discovered a master's thesis on its vegetation, by one Shirley Larmour, published in 1974. Obtaining a copy through the University of British Columbia's electronic archives, I devoured the thesis in a single sitting. Larmour had established and monitored a whole series of square plots, following an elevation gradient upward. The project was an impressive documentation of all the plant species she encountered. I got very excited at the mention of vegetation plots and the possibility of relocating and remonitoring them. "Longitudinal trajectories" is our name for this kind of data, the holy grail of vegetation ecologists. So I tracked Shirley down, now a church organist in Regina, Saskatchewan. She had a good laugh when I mentioned her thesis project. "My kids think I did that work when dinosaurs still roamed the earth," she said.

Unfortunately, Shirley said the plots she put in were temporary, not permanently marked, and done long before the days of GPS. Even so, on my walks I always keep a sharp eye out for old wooden stakes.

Laurie Rockwell, now passed, was a volunteer warden on TCER. He was also a serious birder, recording bird sightings on his visits. His list includes eighty-three different species. This is remarkable, since there is no water anywhere except far down in the inaccessible canyon, so that eliminates a host of riparian and water birds. Colleagues of Laurie said his record of sightings is not a testimony to TCER's resident avian diversity, but to the endless hours that he spent there.

Laurie and I also took Shirley's original plant list and established it as a baseline. Over the years, he and I were able to add several species to it. At this writing, the list stands at one hundred and forty-four. As for mammals, I have seen mule deer there, coyotes and the aforementioned bears, who are absolutely, stunningly black. Whenever I see one of these bears, normally motionless and at a distance, the landscape is instantly transformed into a colour photograph with a jet-black, bear-shaped hole cut into it. As observant as I am when on TCER, the bears always see me before I see them.

Shirley's 1974 work showed a substantial presence of diffuse knapweed, but on my walks I rarely see it now, thanks to biocontrol. Another invasive, Dalmatian toadflax, is moderately abundant, but when I take a close look at these weeds I often see the little black weevils that were introduced as toadflax biocontrol agents in the early 1990s. That always cheers me up. Another obvious invasive is yellow salsify, whose flowers turn into giant puffballs of floating seeds, like a dandelion on steroids. No biocontrol agents have yet been introduced for this plant. Yellow salsify is a tall, single-stemmed plant. In early summer, its developing flower head is right at waist level, perfect for casual decapitation as I walk along.

If I happen to finish a visit down at TCER's lower end and am feeling lazy, I will sometimes walk back to my car along the edge of the back nine. Whenever I do this, I am struck by how the golf course is a kind of simulacrum of the pre-contact landscape: widely scattered mature ponderosas, limbed up (by chainsaw in this case) to twenty metres or more, a few chosen shrubs here and there, no juvenile trees, and abundant grass. I watch the mostly male golfers as they make their way through this artificial landscape. They talk freely, and the adjacent canyon wall amplifies their voices. They josh with each other and swing their arms, exhibiting a sense of

The Sky and the Patio

physical and mental well-being. Golf is partly responsible for this state of mind, but I believe the main source is the landscape itself. However engineered this back nine may be, it carries traces of the ur-landscape, the forest's edge, the parkland, the veldt, the landscape where humans evolved, the one we made natural.

Some of the rocks on TCER are quite sittable, inviting you (after you check around the base for rattlesnakes) to sit and slip into reverie, study your notes, decide where to go next, or eat your sandwich. Some, like the Touching Rock, are relatively smooth glacial erratics that were shaped and moved about by Pleistocene ice sheets. They are free-standing, and the nicest to sit upon. Others are brittle, sharp-edged and eruptive fragments poking out of the ground, clearly volcanic in origin. Any loose rocks that are suitcase-sized or smaller get moved every spring by hungry bears searching for ants. Up at the foot of the reserve's steepest terrain is an unsittable and even unwalkable scree slope of broken rock. All of this fierce, unchanging geology stands in mute contrast to the slow and elegant dynamism of their companions the trees, the shrubs and the grasses.

My second-favourite rock after the Touching Rock stands about head-high and is a heavily fractured conglomerate that looks like it came out of the volcanic oven too soon. There is a shallow basin on top of the rock, and growing out of it is a healthy, mature saskatoon shrub. Who knows how many eons of lichen decomposition, ashfall and windblown silt it took to create a fertile niche for this saskatoon? No doubt its roots have found bits of water and nourishment deep in the rock's fractures. Somehow this shrub and its rock bring the disparate worlds of geology and botany into an inspiring and harmonious whole. Now it is up to me to do the same with golf and ecology.

22
A NAGGING WISH FOR THE DIVINE

LOCAL HISTORY INTERSECTS with world history, and there are entanglements. As a resident of our small town, I was casually aware of the family surname Logie, since a local road bears that name. This fact was a mere cipher until I stumbled upon a reference to one Jack Logie, and his highly alliterative "Summerland Social Issues Summer School" from the 1920s. This school, I discovered, taught a melange of mysticism, arts and crafts, trade unionism and socialism. Wow. Right here? In my conservative, bucolic, sleepy town, which would have been a mere village back in the '20s?

Of course, I was hooked and dove right in.

The Logie story actually begins in 1831, in the town Yekaterinoslav, in southern Russia, when one Helena Blavatsky is born. Growing up, Madame Blavatsky masters several languages, then travels to India and to England, writes prolifically and pioneers a new religious movement called Theosophy. This new religious torch gets handed off to an Englishwoman named Annie Besant (1847–1933), a prolific writer, traveller to India, avid supporter of women's rights, and adoptive mother of young Jiddu Krishnamurti. Besant travels to New York and gives lectures, thus triggering the formation of the American Theosophical movement. Shortly after that, a Canadian chapter is born.

Theosophy, which persists to this day, is very difficult to pin down. Its doctrines range from the rational to the occult, with many stops in between. The three Declared Objects of the Theosophical Society are:

To form a nucleus of the universal brotherhood of humanity, without distinction of race, creed, sex, caste or color.

To encourage the comparative study of religion, philosophy, and science.

To investigate unexplained laws of nature and the powers latent in humanity.

Theosophy, like other religions, is rife with code words and ideological constructs. One of them, the Order of the Star in the East, surrounds young Krishnamurti. The religion also juggles some very diverse ideas: trade unionism, the Sixth Root Race, social activism, Shambhala, the astral plane and karma. I was sure that we baby boomers had invented karma in the '60s, but go figure.

Enter Jack Logie. Born in Manitoba in 1881, he trains as a pharmacist, moves to Summerland and at the tender age of twenty opens a pharmacy. Diminutive, with a bad leg as a result of a childhood illness, Logie dives into community affairs with relentless energy. A talented musician, he forms the Summerland Brass and Reed Band. He becomes a noble grand of the Odd Fellows, reads poetry, leads young people on hikes into the mountains and studies local Indigenous culture.

As the Great Depression sets in, Logie becomes concerned about the number of his fellow townspeople who languish in poverty. Influenced by the rising tide of socialist and Marxist thought, he decides to take action, inviting poor townsfolk to create handicrafts for sale. Under his leadership, a group starts making pottery, wood carvings and basketry. Logie goes on to build a log cabin adjacent to the main road where the crafters can work and sell their wares to travellers. Certainly, this is no panacea, but the craft store gives unemployed locals a bit of income and, perhaps more importantly, shows them the value of direct action.

Meanwhile, this newfangled not-quite-religion called Theosophy has reached the wilds of the British Columbia Interior. It is a natural for Logie, and he starts a congregation.

Local intersections with movements in the wider world are often aided by the ganglia of art. Logie embraces Theosophy simultaneously with Canadian painters Arthur Lismer, Frederick Varley and Lawren Harris, of Group of Seven fame. In turn, Lawren Harris introduces painter Emily Carr to Theosophy.

But back to Logie. In 1922, Jack starts his Social Issues Summer School at the aforesaid log cabin, which runs for ten days each summer. Tents and cots are made available to out-of-towners, and featured speakers come from all over Canada. Topics range from arts, music and economics to Marxism, poetry, theatre, pottery and, of course, Theosophy. A prominent visiting speaker is Reverend J.S. Woodsworth, the iconic Canadian social activist and founder of the Cooperative Commonwealth Federation (CCF), the progenitor of the New Democratic Party.

Meanwhile, a group of Theosophists start the Aquarian Foundation on some forested land near Nanaimo, on Vancouver Island. They are led by the English mystic Edward Wilson, also known as Brother XII. Wilson becomes adept at getting donations from wealthy society ladies to support his foundation, which soon morphs into a highly toxic cult of personality. Storm clouds, and the RCMP, gather. When things come to a head in 1932, Wilson absconds in a tugboat with all the money, never to be seen again.

Fortunately, Jack Logie is completely immune to the temptations of personality cults, but he is definitely attracted to Theosophy. After four successful years with his summer school, he converts it to Besant College, the Western Canada branch of the World Theosophical University. The college's aim is to "apply the Ancient Wisdom to the problems of modern life." Meanwhile, he maintains his multifarious interests, but something prompts him to leave Summerland. This may be due to the opinions of the local conservative press and business leaders, who are not enamoured with Jack's political activism. Or the mounting weight of the

Depression. Or a growing fascination with Theosophy. At any rate, his diary, which is held by the Summerland Museum, offers this brief comment: "December 3, 1929, left for Ojai."

A small California town in semi-desert country northeast of Los Angeles, Ojai is one of the world capitals of Theosophy, a mecca for seekers of various persuasions, and would become the set for Frank Capra's 1937 film *Lost Horizon*. It is also the home of Krishnamurti, the adopted son of Annie Besant, who is chosen to become the world teacher and guru of Theosophy.

During his year at Ojai, Logie works as a groundskeeper at Krotona, the Theosophy headquarters, and spends time with Krishnamurti. In late 1929, Krishnamurti travels to Europe, and at a momentous outdoor gathering in Holland, he renounces his connection to Theosophy. He then moves on to a notable career as an independent thinker, philosopher, writer and lecturer.

Logie returns to British Columbia and eventually settles in Victoria, where he continues his activism, but like Krishnamurti, he has also moved on from Theosophy. In 1932, he is able to convince the then world-renowned Krishnamurti to come to Victoria to deliver a lecture.

Jack Logie's log cabin still stands. I pass it every time I go from our home down to Okanagan Lake, and it reminds me that synthesis is possible: arts, politics, philosophy and crafts can occasionally cross over, to mutual benefit.

Putting aside all the occultist astral/sixth-race woo-woo bullshit, Theosophy does offer something to this lifelong but pining atheist: the notion of a secular divine. That God is actually composed of humans and nature, together. But perhaps secular divine is a contradiction. What I am looking for is a religion without gods or churches, one that embraces ecstasy in nature, human companionship and wine. One of my colleagues suggests dropping "divine" and going with "the secular sublime" instead, thereby conveying the notion of elevated, ecstatic feelings without reference to divinity.

Curiously, Immanuel Kant defined the sublime as our rational superiority over nature, but I'm not buying his definition. The opposite of sublime is the word *subliminal*, meaning a mental process occurring below the threshold of sensation or consciousness. Some of the processes that generate our sense of ecstasy in nature do slip in unawares, so I'm not buying that definition either.

Every time I pass Summerland's Logie Road, I think of Jack, a very grounded spirit wrestler, fallen Theosophist, and role model — at least for me.

The Theosophists do believe in a secular heaven. Coincidentally, it is called Summerland.

23
MYTHMAKING ON THE SIMILKAMEEN

THERE IS A demographic of mostly older white males who chase earthly secrets. These are the gold-panners, the hunters, the rockhounds, the amateur archaeologists, the cryptobiologists. Their quests to discover and unravel those secrets involve maps, trails, archival searches, intense communications with equally smitten colleagues and weekend explorations. The unrevealed secrets they chase can become lore. The lore can then morph to legend, and ultimately, to myth. Witness the twenty-point buck, the lost gold mine, the sasquatch, the Ogopogo. Mythmaking is not a recent phenomenon: the ancient Greeks were masters of the genre. Our modern myths are generally harmless, and can even have a positive role. Let me explain.

Some geographies are very ordinary and unromantic. Tevye laments this about his humdrum little village of Anatevka. What, he asks rhetorically, does it have?

A little bit of this, a little bit of that.

A pot, a pan, a broom, a hat.

Local myths can give unique character to otherwise ordinary places, and provide fodder for citizen pride.

Almost by definition, a myth is equal parts fact and fabrication. The line between myth and legend is blurry, but both forms rely on seekers, curators and the passage of time. Neither one self-generates; both require an original human storyteller, a Tevye. Then subsequent curators of the story step in. These curators must not only preserve: they are duty-bound to modify, misinterpret, extend and add supporting detail. This accumulation of detail and detour is necessary in order to elevate story to lore, lore to legend, and finally, legend to myth.

On the settler side, my South Okanagan–Similkameen region of British Columbia is woefully short of myths. We don't have a sasquatch, an Ogopogo or a Lost Lemon gold mine. No lost cities, no alien landing sites. We do, however, have a local story and potential legend known as the Spanish Mound of the Similkameen. In the temporal chain of self-appointed curators — as defined above — I am probably ninth or tenth in line. This is good, since passage through many hands guarantees the story will ferment, diversify and bifurcate.

Our candidate myth involves three distinct cultures, the Syilx, the Spanish and the Settler. It embraces several locations along the Similkameen River Valley, and connects either to the mouth of the Columbia River or to contemporary New Mexico, depending on your interpretation. The story's time span is either three centuries or five, and it can be told either backwards or forwards.

The central artifact of this fledgling myth is an enigmatic and fascinating pictograph. The Similkameen Valley hosts a number of Indigenous pictographs, perhaps due to its closeness to the Tulameen ochre beds (ochre is a rare red clay that was prized as a durable paint for pictographs). The pictograph in question, near the small town of Hedley, is locally known as "the prisoner painting." It shows four human figures walking single file. A straight, heavy line connects all four figures by the neck. Adjacent to the four figures are three dog-like creatures, also walking in the same direction. Nearby is another pictograph of a person mounted on a horse. This rider's head is outsized in comparison to the rest of his body, possibly indicating a hat of some sort. The dates of these pictographs are not known. Out of the curatorial haze, the following story emerges, offering one explanation.

A group of Spaniards, all mounted on horseback, arrive in the Similkameen. A battle ensues, and the Spaniards take several Indigenous prisoners. Time passes and the Spaniards decamp, heading north to the present-day city of Kelowna. There, they construct a large building near the current Orchard Park Shopping Centre, as winter quarters for themselves and their horses. After a period of time, they return to the Similkameen, but the local Syilx ambush them and massacre them all. They bury the corpses of the Spaniards, together with their weapons and armour, in a mound near the present-day town of Olalla.

These are the bare bones of the story, likely first recounted by a Syilx elder to a curious settler, no one knows exactly when. Many intriguing story details and variants have been added over time, by various curators.

The truly fascinating part of the story is the Spanish connection. Where did these Spaniards come from? Where did they acquire the horses? When did this event happen?

Early Spanish incursions into the Americas were chronicles of incredible persistence, insatiable greed for gold, and horrendous brutality. The early exploits of Pizarro, Cortés and Coronado are well known. Later, there were a number of Spanish seagoing expeditions up the Pacific Coast, as far as Vancouver Island and beyond. But there are no verified historical records of early Spaniards travelling through the Okanagan-Similkameen. So where did these clandestine hombres come from?

One explanation is that sometime in the mid-1700s a Spanish galleon shipwrecked at the mouth of the Columbia River, and some survivors made it ashore. From there, they travelled up the Columbia to the Okanagan River, and eventually to the Similkameen. I like this version, but there are a few problems with it. Where did the horses come from? Were they onboard, and did they swim ashore with the Spaniards? A less difficult problem is why these men chose to come all the way to the Similkameen. Gold and wanderlust were powerful Spanish motivators. Or perhaps the men were searching for the Straits of Anián, the undiscovered waterway that connected the Pacific and Atlantic oceans. That was another powerful myth in its day.

Some curators suggest the oversized head of the man on horseback depicts a metal *morion* helmet typical of the conquistadors. Additionally, old hammered copper plates have been found at Indigenous burial sites in the valley. The suggestion is that these were components of Spanish breastplate armour, or perhaps copies of them. The problem with this theory is that by the 1750s, Spanish warriors had abandoned the use of traditional metal armour and helmets. But then again, maybe these hombres were old-school, and out of touch with current sartorial styles.

The explanation I favour: the Spaniards were actually a group of renegade breakaways from Francisco Coronado's search for the Seven Cities of Cibola, in 1540. These cities were located somewhere north of Mexico and made entirely of gold, and Coronado was desperate to find them. This explanation takes care of not only the armour problem but the horse problem as well, since Coronado's army was mounted. And a Coronado connection does give the story an element of the fabulous.

Somewhere around modern-day Gallup or Santa Fe, a group of Coronado's disgruntled soldiers, now convinced that the Seven Cities is an illusion, sneak away from the expedition in the middle of the night, taking supplies, horses and dogs with them. They make their way northward through present-day Nevada, Oregon and Washington, hell-bent for British Columbia's Similkameen Valley.

But why would they head for the incredibly distant and unknown Similkameen, you might ask? Gold, wanderlust and profoundly erratic human behaviour, I would answer.

Horses do provide an interesting side-story, with mythical proportions as well. Although the common wisdom is horses became extinct in North America at the end of the Ice Age, some argue that they have been here all along. Thus, the first European horses that arrived with Cortés in Mexico in 1615 simply joined their resident equine brethren. The study of horse genetics and bloodlines is a fascinating rabbit hole. Apparently, the early Spanish explorers favoured small horses, since they didn't take up so much room in their crowded galleons.

Several hundred kilometres to the north of the Similkameen, there is another myth in the making. The Brittany Triangle, a remote swampy region in the Chilcotin country west of Williams Lake, is home to a band of feral horses. Some folks claim these horses are direct descendants of the original Spanish mustangs. Because of their remote habitat, they never interbred with other equine strains. But how did they get there? When did they get there? Again, this fact (or strong inference) gives rise to much speculation. Excellent myth potential resides in the bogs of the Brittany.

And where exactly is the Spanish Mound located? Just north of Olalla, some say. Others say no, it is near Keremeos, still others say west of Hedley, or perhaps it is all the way over near Princeton. The broader and vaguer the secret's search area is, the more compelling it becomes.

Could the prisoner pictograph be a modern fake? If it is genuine, could it have simply been misinterpreted? Or did a local Syilx elder make up a fanciful story to explain the pictograph to some credulous settler/curator? Just who was our Tevye?

When you think of it, the complexity of the two elements — pictograph and mound — gives the story credibility. That same complexity helps propel the story toward myth.

I spent some time trying to track down the very first link, the ur-story of this curatorial chain, but I failed. In the end, I don't care. With the Spanish Mound, the South Okanagan–Similkameen finally has a myth to match its mountains.

24
CHOPAKA KILPOOLA KOBAU

THIS JOURNEY STARTS at a dead end just above the little Chopaka Valley. The Nighthawk Crossing, perhaps the sleepiest of all US–Canada border crossings, is visible below me. The only road here, the one I am on, is a single winding dirt track that goes nowhere. Nowhere, in the sense that it does not connect with any other road: Chopaka is definitely somewhere. Farther up the Canadian side of this valley is a prominent stone. Geologists would call it a glacial erratic, but the stone hosts another story, one that belongs to the Syilx people.

As I begin my extended backtrack from the dead end, heading eastward along the border, I enter a broad, southward-sloping plateau, also known as Chopaka. The nearest towns are distant Osoyoos to the east and Cawston to the north. This Chopaka plateau is perhaps better described as an apron, whose strings are tied to Black Mountain. The lower hem is the Similkameen River, just across the line. That river, after looping southward on the Canadian side, crosses into Washington State and turns abruptly east, closely tracking the borderline.

This Chopaka apron is covered by a dense carpet of waist-high Wyoming big sagebrush. Even though it is just a few kilometres wide and long, the uniformity of the grey sagebrush stand makes the apron seem vast. Perhaps that sense is amplified by expansive views down to the Similkameen's valley, and then way off to the west, where the Cathedral Range looms. Other than a cattle fence and Monument 113, a concrete pillar marking the border, no human structures are visible.

The Sky and the Patio

Why am I on this three-part, uphill journey? Let me count the ways: tourist, ecologist, fence contractor, solitary wanderer, expat, bather. Immersing myself in this last undisturbed, low-elevation and northernmost fragment of the Great Basin biome. Chopaka is a haven for species at risk, and for the hard-bitten biologists who track them. There are three grazing exclosures here, and I am botanically intimate with each of them. Chopaka offers me a view across to my former country, the United States, and to my former home in Okanogan County. That triggers a contradictory mixture of nostalgia and political anger.

Proceeding eastward again, I pass through two dry coulees angling downward from Black Mountain. In the second coulee there is an old concrete foundation. At one time, in the 1920s, fifteen settler families lived along this road; now there are none. The foundation is a relic from that era, a profoundly ill-advised hog operation, thirty kilometres by rough wagon road to the nearest market. These and other failed early settlements in remote parts of Western Canada can be traced back to the federal government and the Canadian Pacific Railway, who jointly created an elaborate fantasy and inducement to "go west, young man," (by rail, of course), where you would surely find a new and self-sufficient farming life.

Moving farther east, past Chopaka and a little higher in elevation, I enter Kilpoola country. Its namesake lake is well known to adventurous fly fishers. Kilpoola is sweetwater, but just a few kilometres beyond it is another waterbody, Blue Lake.

There are four well-known saline lakes in the South Okanagan: White, Mahoney, Spotted and Blue. Each one has unique chemical properties, making them priority destinations for roving limnologists. A sweetwater lake has roughly the same water chemistry from surface to bottom: Blue Lake, on the other hand, has a sharp division. Midway down its water column is an abrupt change in salinity, and the two layers are meromictic: they never mix. The waters of Blue are too saline for fish, but moderate enough to host a stunning variety of invertebrates, amphibians, reptiles and birds.

The north end of Blue Lake is a broad, shallow bay, part of a BC government protected area. The bay has been traditionally used by cattle for drinking and loafing. As a result, the vegetation and habitats in and around the bay were trashed. I was fortunate to be part of a diverse group that came together to tackle the problem. Representatives from two different government ministries, the local First Nation, the ranching community, professional biologists and naturalists temporarily suspended various long-standing disagreements to come up with a plan to reclaim the bay. At first, the solution seemed straightforward: fence out the bay, and at the same time create a narrow fenced laneway that gives cattle access to drinking water but not to the rest of the bay.

Things were looking good, but then biologists weighed in, informing us that two species at risk, the spadefoot and the tiger salamander, are known to hibernate underground along the shores of Blue Lake. Not only that, in the heat of summer these two amphibians frequently burrow into the ground close to the shoreline, to stay cool. Besides being rare in Canada, both are quite fascinating: the spadefoot is neither frog nor toad, but claims intermediate status, and the tiger salamander has a lurid life history, worthy of Greek mythology.

This news dropped a big amphibian wrench into our plan. For weeks I was plagued by visions of driving fenceposts into the ground and skewering spadefoots or maiming salamanders. I thought maybe we could pick a time to fence, after winter hibernation but before the heat of summer, and have a team of consulting amphibian experts physically inspect each spot of ground just before the fenceposts were pounded in. While working out the costs and logistics of this plan, I received an unexpected phone call: the two government ministries in charge of the area had come to an agreement to retire the Blue Lake parcel from active grazing tenure.

This little bay is popular with birds, as well as with hardcore birders. Some 140 different avian species have been identified here, a truly remarkable number given the remoteness of the site.

The Sky and the Patio

Hard by the Blue Lake bay stands a magnificent veteran ponderosa pine. I took some measurements and realized the tree would place among the top twenty of its ponderosa peers in the University of British Columbia's BigTree Registry. This is surprising, since much of Chopaka and Kilpoola consists of dry sagelands, but there is a terrain break right at Blue Lake. The prevailing southerly aspect gives way here to rocky, undulating ridgeline terrain, supporting patches of forest here and there. One of those undulations contains a pocket of moist, very fertile soil where this magnificent veteran had found its niche. After I had carefully measured the tree's circumference with a tape measure, I could not resist embracing it. My wingspan is rather large — thirty-six-inch shirtsleeves are still a bit short — but I could barely hug a third of the trunk.

This big tree is part of what I call a council grove: a group of veteran trees that tower above an open understory of shrubs, grasses and mosses. Ponderosa council groves are found here and there in the Southern Interior, and they create a quiet, thoughtful environment. Sunlight filters downward, highlighting the brick-red puzzle bark of the massive tree trunks. The trees silently encourage us to sit down on the soft, cushiony duff, dispel the dross of the day, and engage our collective wisdom. Perhaps a mourning cloak butterfly will flit about in totally still air. The trees' own wisdom has created this enduring council community, and they offer it to us as a template.

What do these pines, spadefoots, sockeyes and grasses expect of me? How do I do right by them? How should I live my life, knowing they are watching? Learn their life cycles, and speak out on their behalf. Compost, perhaps. Compost and recycle. Deal with my carbon footprint. Build local community. Look after grandkids. Encourage the arts.

Farther along the road is the Turtle Pond, another small waterbody badly abused by livestock. For years it hosted a thriving population of domestic goldfish. On my trips by the pond, I would always stop to watch these critters and speculate on the possible motive of the person who brought them there.

Heading north and downslope now, toward Highway 3, the Crowsnest. The track I am on is gazetted as the Kruger Mountain Road, named after Theodore Kruger, a German settler who manned the Hudson's Bay trading post at Keremeos for a time in the 1860s. As I approach Highway 3, this rutted track becomes gravel and finally pavement as it passes through a classic Okanagan spaghetti suburb of newer homes and acreages.

Briefly onto Highway 3 heading west, I pass otherworldly kłlilx'w, or Spotted Lake. The bottom of this shallow, alkaline waterbody consists of a series of perfectly concentric two-metre-wide circles. The water colour in each circle can be slightly different from the circles next to it. I have never counted them, but locals say there is a circle for each day of the year. This lake, sacred to the Syilx Nation, was owned privately for decades until 2001, when the Okanagan Nation Alliance reclaimed ownership.

Just beyond the lake is the Richter Pass, a low divide that separates the Okanagan and Similkameen river systems. Richter is one of several early settler surnames associated with this region: Richter (from Austria), Kruger (Germany), Barcelo (Mexico), Cawston (Ontario), Haynes (Ireland), Ellis (England) and Allison (England). All were involved in cattle ranching. Susan Allison and John Haynes ("the hanging judge") were polar opposites: Allison befriended and worked with local Indigenous folks; Haynes stole their land.

Our settler history of the Okanagan-Similkameen is basically one of exploitation. Initially, it was a corridor for the transport of Hudson's Bay Company furs as they were moved from the Interior to Fort Astoria and then on to Europe. Bought for tokens, the furs sold for kings' ransoms to European fashionistas. That was the first of many assaults on British Columbia's furbearers. Then came gold. Something for nothing. Thousands of clamouring Americans, who had missed out on California's 1849 gold rush, headed north. The Fraser Canyon and the Cariboo were major destinations, but many desperate men pounced on local strikes in Princeton, Tulameen, Allenby, Hedley, Fairview, Greenwood, Rock Creek and other locations. Chinese miners, satisfied with simply making a living instead of a killing, moved in to work the claims as they petered out. The town of Fairview in its gold mining heyday featured an elegant three-storey Tudor-style hotel; now not a single building remains. What was once a boom town is now grass and sagebrush.

On the heels of the gold rush came cattle ranching. Hungry miners wanted beef, and we were happy to oblige. A curious ecological oversight — extensive grasslands with few native grazers — became an extravagant gift to the new cattle barons. Then came a somewhat less exploitative era of small-scale farming and ranching, but which also witnessed the birth of overheated and overhyped land development schemes. The Okanagan was literally marketed as the "British Garden of Eden." Next was the petrochemical bonanza, or in the words of Kurt Vonnegut, "thermodynamic whoopee." No oil and gas is produced in these two valleys, but we do our best here to consume this paleological windfall. Next came cheap Chinese consumer goods — something for almost nothing. Every morning, as I put on my underpants, I confront the tag *Made in China*. In the current era, we are deeply immersed in another exploitation: real estate. Karl Marx had a much more descriptive two-word term for this activity: unearned increment.

Stay tuned for the next big Something For Nothing.

Just to the west of the Richter Pass, I turn off onto a gravel road. Although now badly washboarded, this Mount Kobau road is beautifully engineered, truly the opposite of the gnarly, 4WD-only Kruger Mountain Road. The Kobau road was built in the mid-'60s for the proposed Queen Elizabeth II astronomical observatory, and it gains more than a thousand metres in altitude over its twenty-kilometre run. At some point, astronomical politics intervened and the observatory was never built, but the durable Kobau road remains. If I were to map my tripartite journey, the Chopaka-Kilpoola portion would be a kind of random scribble, and the Kobau portion a series of graceful loops. As I start up the road, I am in pure sagebrush country, but soon it transitions to ponderosa, and then on to Douglas-fir. A large stand of blackened, dead trees is a reminder of the aggressive Testalinden wildfire of 2015. Nearing the summit, I enter graceful stands of Engelmann spruce and subalpine fir. Finally topping out, I am back into sagebrush, but this is a unique high-elevation variety known as Vasey's sage.

The Syilx name for this mountain is *Txasqin*; no one knows for sure where the settler place name *Kobau* originated. One theory is that the geologist George Mercer Dawson assigned the name during his explorations here in the 1870s. There seems to be no antecedent: the place name of Kobau is not found anywhere else in the world, nor does any famous person bear that surname. *Kobau* does represent the number nine in ancient Chaldean numerology, a system that connects numbers to letters. It is said that when everything is perfectly aligned in the mystical Chaldean system, the letters vibrate. Geologist Dawson was widely read, and privately a bit of a mystic, so the Chaldean explanation for this mountain's name is quite possible. However, the true answer remains in our very small regional basket of mystery and lore.

At 1,870 metres, Kobau is a minor peak by Canadian standards, but it stands quietly alone, towering over its two low-elevation valleys. Once on the summit, eyes and mind wander from the Kettle Range to the east, over to the Cascades to the south and on to the Cathedrals to the west. After a good look downward into the Okanagan Valley, a few meandering steps over to the western edge of the summit and the Similkameen Valley comes into view. Even though Kobau stands well above the surrounding mountains, it has a similar configuration. Okanagan-Similkameen mountains are not craggy, they are voluptuous.

The Kobau summit is one of the best dark sky preserves in southern Canada, and it hosts an annual week-long Star Party, attracting astronomical geeks from far and wide. They look upward, for knowledge and meaning and joy. As an ecological geek I tend to look down, for the same reasons. In the words of the eminently quotable historian Simon Schama, mine is a "vegetable theology." Schama also describes the almost universal connection between altitude and beatitude. He shows that virtually every culture has

The Sky and the Patio

examples of mountain sojourners seeking spirituality, blessedness, humility, timelessness or some other lofty sentiment, upon a summit.

My own sojourn toward a mountain bond is a perilously narrow one. To one side of my very narrow path is Syilx knowledge and culture; to the other side is religion. As honourable as these two worldviews are, they are out of bounds for this honky agnostic settler. Thus, I must tread a very personal path, making it up as I go along, from random bits of ecology, literature and introspection. Many of the words I use while struggling to define a personal nature bond have traditional religious connotations. Spirituality, humility, transcendence, sublimity, epiphany: these and similar words are co-opted. This makes my path to defining and creating a bond even more tortuous.

Chopaka, Kilpoola, Kobau. It is a journey, and a mantra. A complex line passing from valley bottom to mid-elevation to mountain top. The heart of the future Okanagan-Similkameen National Park Reserve. An odd ecological circle, from sagebrush to sagebrush. Three humble places, each with traces of the eternal and the divine.

Our settler history plays a very minor role as we wrestle with today's crises. In part, this is because there are no obvious precedents for climate change, petrochemical dependency, pollution, global pandemics, opioid addictions, overpopulation and so on. Another factor is the total focus on the present moment, brought on by the overwhelming immediacy of cellphones and digital communication. Taken together, it is no surprise that our local history seems irrelevant, but it is not. We have a complex and ambiguous past to confront.

Up until now, we Okanagan-Similkameen settlers are here for a good time, not a long time. I hope we can change that. Chopaka, Kilpoola and Kobau stand ready to help, if we stop merely taking and begin giving back.

25
PATIO ADIEU

It is a fall evening. Days are foreshortened now, and the leaves of the Coronation grapevine are just beginning to turn. The sky is in that luminous phase just before sunset. The few clouds are reflecting muted colours of pink, orange and scarlet. A passenger jet contrail overhead shows me the declination between Vancouver and Calgary. Reluctant to declare an end to the patio season, I have dressed warmly for tonight's meal. The main is a chicken curry, with onions, homegrown carrots and that humblest of garden vegetables, rutabaga. I have paired it with a Meritage red blend from a South Asian winery near Oliver. This homemade curry of mine is a pale shadow of those served in the many excellent South Asian restaurants up and down the valley, but it does pay homage to their wonderful and varied cuisine.

South Asian immigrants began arriving in BC in the very early 1900s and, like the Chinese, were subject to all manner of exclusionary laws until well after World War II. Beginning in the 1960s, South Asian folks found opportunities here in agriculture, starting fruit orchards, vegetable cropping and, more recently, vineyards. To our great benefit, they also opened ethnic restaurants and food stands up and down these two valleys. The chronological progression of Okanagan-Similkameen ethnic restaurants is interesting to track: first came the Italian, then Greek, then Chinese. Next came the South Asian and now, more recently, Japanese. The South Asian restaurants give us the chance to explore dozens of dishes and their regional variants. One of my restaurant favourites

The Sky and the Patio

is the spicy, deep-fried cauliflower, which raises a very pedestrian vegetable to culinary heights.

As I consume my amateur curry and the excellent Meritage, I am rereading Loren Eiseley's 1970 book *The Invisible Pyramid*. Eiseley was an anthropologist, naturalist, mystic and deep thinker, taking the long view of the human species. Eiseley's "first world" was that of nature, before the emergence of humans. Now occupying the "second world," the mutable domain of thought, humans question their right to be there, and yet fear a return to the first world. As children, Eiseley and his friends played in a dense thicket of native sunflowers, and he uses this experience as an analogy; that "sunflower forest" of his childhood was the first world.

Writing at the dawn of the Space Age and the pre-dawn of climate change, Eiseley had a pessimistic, and somewhat prophetic, view of humanity:

> Modern man, the world eater, respects no space and no thing green or furred as sacred. The march of the machines has entered his blood. They are his seed boxes, his potential wings and guidance systems on the far roads of the universe. The fruition time of the planet virus is at hand. It is high autumn, the autumn before winter topples the spore cities.

Eiseley's "planet virus" was technology in general. It is safe to say that today's version of the planet virus is our favourite technology subset: internal combustion of oil and gas and the subsequent release of carbon dioxide. The western world has generally recognized climate change as a planetary crisis for a couple of decades now, but basic human psychology dictates that if a "crisis" carries on for twenty or thirty years, we no longer view it as a crisis. So as a result we are concerned, but complacent. We are programmed to respond to local catastrophes, not the gradual erosion of an entire planet.

It is a long evening and I have brought along a second book, a collection of poems by the Chilean leftist politician-poet Pablo

Neruda. In his poem "Oda al Vino" ("Ode to Wine"), he places the beverage squarely at the centre of our human experience:

> Day-colored wine,
> night-colored wine,
> wine with purple feet
> or wine with topaz blood,
> wine,
> starry child
> of earth,
> wine, smooth
> as a golden sword,
> soft
> as lascivious velvet,
> wine, spiral-seashelled
> and full of wonder,
> amorous,
> marine;
> never has one goblet contained you,
> one song, one man,
> you are choral, gregarious,
> at the least, you must be shared.

This Meritage I am drinking is a blend of four different grapes. If Pablo were still with us, I am sure he would approve.

Blending of different grape varieties was traditionally forbidden in the varietal wine industry, but innovative winemakers grew restless under that restriction. Finally, in the 1980s, the Meritage designation was inaugurated. A red Meritage may be vinted from a blend of any of the eight classic Bordeaux varieties, including Cabernet Sauvignon, Merlot, Cabernet Franc and Malbec.

I like this notion of blending, sharing and experimentation. It suits my style. I intend to keep on doing that with literature, food, wine, gardening, grape growing and nature exploration. In between I will compost, cut firewood, ride my bicycle, play with grandchildren, vote, support mass transit and go to climate change

The Sky and the Patio

events. I refuse to become a rose-coloured Pollyanna, nor will I be a disillusioned defeatist. I will find that middle ground, somewhere between the sky and the patio.

Suggested Reading

(Note: this is not by any means a full bibliography. I have not cited those well-known works that would be easily available via libraries or bookstores.)

The Sky and the Patio
Jorge Luis Borges, *Selected Poems* 1923–1967 (Delacorte Press, 1972).

The Army of Five Hundred
www.omafra.gov.on.ca/english/crops/facts/info_sjwbeetles.htm.

Andrew Douglass and Dendropyrochronology
James H. Speer, *Fundamentals of Tree-Ring Research* (University of Arizona Press, 2010).

Eocene Walk
George Mercer Dawson's voluminous writings can be accessed online at: archivalcollections.library.mcgill.ca/index.php/george-mercer-dawson-papers.

The Metasequoia Mystery:
landscapearchitecturemagazine.org/2016/01/19/the-metasequoia-mystery/.

Sagebrush, Science and Shifting Mosaics
Leonard Marchand and Matt Hughes, *Breaking Trail* (Caitlin Press, 2000).

Compost Fetishism and the Dirty Dozen
Roberta Parish et al., Plants of Southern Interior British Columbia and the Inland Northwest (Partners Publishing, 2018).

Cowboy Dreams

Will James, *Smoky the Cowhorse* (Charles Scribner's Sons, 1926).

Wallace Stegner, *Wolf Willow* (Penguin Classics, 2000).

Thelma Poirier, *Grasslands: The Private Hearings* (Coteau Books, 1990).

A Paean to the Sockeye

Michael Healey, "Resilient Salmon, Resilient Fisheries for British Columbia, Canada" (2009), www.researchgate.net/profile/Michael-Healey-3/publication/285278940_Resilient_salmon/links/5a383732a6fdccdd41fdeb52/Resilient-salmon.pdf?origin=publication_detail.

Gillian Larkin and Pat Slaney, "Implications of Trends in Marine-Derived Nutrient Influx to South Coastal British Columbia Salmonid Production" (1997), citeseerx.ist.psu.edu/viewdoc/download?doi=10.1.1.475.7650&rep=rep1&type=pdf.

Shambala, Feminization and Great Green Furballs

Don Gayton, "Vietnam, Canada and the Draft" (2021), https://dongayton.ca/category/blog/page/2/.

Places of Attachment

Richard Mack and John Thompson, "Evolution in Steppe with Few Large Hooved Mammals" (1982), www.journals.uchicago.edu/doi/abs/10.1086/283953.

Don Gayton, "Native and Non-Native Plant Species in Grazed Grasslands of British Columbia's Southern Interior" (2004), jem-online.org/index.php/jem/article/view/291/210.

Suggested Reading

Chinook Wawa
George Gibbs, *Dictionary of the Chinook Jargon* (Cramoisy Press, 1863), www.washington.edu/uwired/outreach/cspn/Website/Classroom%20Materials/Curriculum%20Packets/Treaties%20&%20Reservations/Documents/Chinook_Dictionary_Abridged.pdf.

Johann Wolfgang von Goethe and the Bee Balm
Nancy Holmes, *The Flicker Tree* (Ronsdale Press, 2012).

The Singularity of Frivolous Purpose
James Young and Charles Clements, *Purshia: The Wild and Bitter Roses* (University of Nevada Press, 2002).

E-Flora BC: Electronic Atlas of the Flora of British Columbia, ibis.geog.ubc.ca/biodiversity/eflora/mobile_index2.html.

The Enduring Pleasures of the Woodstove
Stanley Kauffmann, *Figures of Light: Film Criticism and Comment* (Harper & Row, 1971).

Turtle Naivete
Holling Clancy Holling, *Minn of the Mississippi* (Clarion Books, 1951).

BC Species and Ecosystems Explorer, www2.gov.bc.ca/gov/content/environment/plants-animals-ecosystems/conservation-data-centre/explore-cdc-data/species-and-ecosystems-explorer.

The Natural History of the Bookshelf
William Irwin Thompson, *At the Edge of History* (Harper & Row, 1971) and *The Time Falling Bodies Take to Light* (St. Martin's Press, 1981).

Simon Schama, *Landscape and Memory* (Random House, 1995).

Christopher Alexander, *A Pattern Language* (Oxford University Press, 1977).

The Pantheon of Dusty Heroes
William Lewis and Naojiro Murakami, eds., *Ranald MacDonald: A Narrative of His Life 1824–1894* (Oregon Historical Society Press, 1990).

Climate Change
Jane Jacobs, *The Death and Life of Great American Cities* (Modern Library, 1961).

Aliens, Golf and the Trout Creek Ecological Reserve
Don Gayton, "Documenting Fire History in a British Columbia Ecological Reserve" (2012), jem-online.org/index.php/jem/article/view/161/485.

Chopaka Kilpoola Kobau
See Dawson reference above.

Patio Adieu
Loren Eiseley, *The Invisible Pyramid* (Charles Scribner's Sons, 1970).

Pablo Neruda, *Selected Poems* (Jonathan Cape, 1970).

Acknowledgements

The author gratefully acknowledges the professionalism of the New Star staff and the invaluable editorial assistance of Adrienne Kerr.